Silent Wealth Killers: The Overlooked Habits That Keep You Broke

By: Patrice Shabazz

This is a work of [fiction/nonfiction]. Names, characters, places, and incidents are the product of the author's imagination or are used in a transformative and educational context. Any resemblance to actual persons, living or dead, or actual events is purely coincidental unless otherwise noted.

For permission requests, contact:
Patrice Shabazz
Email: patriceshabazz39@gmail.com
Publisher: Exclusive Heights

ISBN: 978-1-969629-75-4
First Edition: 2025

Cover art by Patrice Shabazz
Printed in the United States of America

Disclaimer

This book is not here to comfort you. It is here to expose you.

If you came looking for watered-down "financial tips," budgeting charts, or a friendly lecture about skipping lattes, close this book now. You won't find that here. What you're holding is a mirror — and the reflection might disgust you. It might make you angry. It might even make you want to slam the book shut. But if you have the courage to keep reading, it could also save your life and your future wealth.

Every word in this book is designed to challenge the lies you've been fed. Society has been engineered to keep you broke — not just through money traps, but through silent killers buried in your daily habits, your environment, your health, and your relationships. These aren't accidents. They're systems. Systems that thrive on your blindness, your obedience, and your distractions.

Nothing here is financial advice in the legal sense. I am not your broker, your banker, or your accountant. I am your wake-up call. Everything written is for educational, cultural, and spiritual empowerment. It is research, observation, parable, and truth — not prescriptions. If you want to sue somebody because the truth cut too deep, sue the system that lied to you, not me.

I write in a style that will offend some, inspire others, and change the few who are ready. Expect profanity. Expect rawness. Expect stories that cross from the boardroom to the block. That's deliberate. Because wealth is not just about spreadsheets — it's about survival, positioning, and power. And to understand power, you must see it from every angle.

If you find yourself uncomfortable, good. Growth lives in discomfort. If you feel exposed, better. That means the killers hiding in your habits are being dragged into the light. If you feel defensive, sit with it. Often the things we defend hardest are the very chains holding us down.

By reading this book, you accept full responsibility for how you process and use this information. You also accept that the biggest threat to your financial future has never been the IRS, the stock market, or your boss — it's been the habits you never thought mattered.

This book is a scalpel. It will cut away illusions. Whether you heal or bleed out depends on your courage to face yourself.

Introduction

Money is not just about numbers. Money is about power, perception, and positioning. You've been taught to think wealth is built on hard work, good jobs, and safe investments. That's the lie. The truth is more dangerous: your future net worth is shaped long before you ever see a paycheck, long before you ever step into a bank, long before you ever hear the words "compound interest."

Your wealth — or lack of it — starts with the invisible killers you've been conditioned to ignore.

This book is about those killers.

Look around. Most people you know are broke, struggling, or one emergency away from disaster. That's not by chance. The system doesn't need a majority of people wealthy. It needs them obedient, consuming, and distracted. So the traps aren't placed in your bank account. They're placed in your lifestyle, your body, your relationships, your identity. They're buried where you'll never think to look.

Think about it: a man who never leaves his house will never collide with opportunity. A woman who carries untreated trauma into every conversation will sabotage deals before they start. A young person loyal to a dead-end job will give away decades of compounding wealth while their boss retires off their back. An unhealthy body, a toxic partner, a weak reputation — these things silently rob more futures than Wall Street ever could.

Yet no one talks about them. Why? Because calling them out would wake too many people up. It's easier to distract you with debates about stocks, side hustles, or "cutting expenses" while ignoring the fact that your inner child still runs your decision-making, or that your digital identity is being weaponized against you, or that your time management is worth more than your hourly wage.

This book tears the mask off.

I'm not here to babysit. I'm here to break things down in the language of the streets and the silence of the boardrooms — because they're playing the same game, just with different pieces. I'll use parables, case studies, psychological research, and raw stories you can't ignore. Each chapter will close with a manifesto, because information without conviction is wasted air.

I want you to read this like your survival depends on it. Because it does.

If you internalize what's written here, you won't just "save money." You'll see the battlefield for what it really is. You'll spot the traps that have kept generations locked in cycles of near-poverty, paycheck slavery, or middle-class stagnation. You'll learn how to maneuver in a world designed to bleed you dry.

By the time you finish, you won't look at life the same. You'll realize that wealth isn't just about making money — it's about protecting your potential from the silent killers that have been eating it alive since the day you were born.

This isn't just a book. It's a scalpel to the illusions that keep you broke. Hold it steady. And don't flinch when it cuts.

Prologue – Negotiation: The First Killer

Every day you negotiate. Whether you admit it or not, whether you prepare for it or not, you're in constant exchanges of power, leverage, and positioning. The question is never if you negotiate — it's how well. Without negotiation skills, you are forever at the mercy of others. You'll pay more, earn less, and give away your value for crumbs. And the brutal truth is this: not having negotiation skills is the silent wealth killer that keeps you stuck begging for fairness in a world that has none.

The Price of Silence

Negotiation shows up everywhere:

Your job salary.

The price of a car.

Rent terms.

The cut in a business deal.

Even date nights, where you negotiate expectations with your partner.

If you don't negotiate, you don't just "miss opportunities." You guarantee yourself the short end of the stick. You put blind faith in the idea that everyone you meet will be fair, generous, and reasonable. That's delusion. In reality, every company, every landlord, every seller, and every gatekeeper is negotiating against you, even if you're too timid to see it.

To enter the world without negotiation skills is like walking into a gladiator arena with no sword. You're not just unprepared — you're prey.

Corporate POV vs. Street POV

Corporate POV: Companies EXPECT employees to negotiate. They lowball salaries, benefits, and promotions precisely because they know most people won't push back. The difference between two employees with the same title could be tens of thousands a year — not based on performance, but on one having the guts to counter-offer. Corporations reward those who know their worth, punish those who don't, and quietly pocket the difference.

Street POV: On the block, negotiation is survival. Hustlers who don't negotiate get cheated by suppliers, shorted by buyers, and robbed by middlemen. Artists who don't negotiate contracts sign away publishing, masters, and likeness for pennies. The label flashes $50,000 cash in front of a kid from the hood, and he gives away rights worth $50 million. That's not a lack of talent. That's a lack of negotiation.

Both arenas prove the same law: without negotiation, you're not a player. You're a product.

The Psychology of Submission

Most people fear negotiation because they fear conflict. Psychologists call this "avoidance behavior" — the brain equates disagreement with danger. People worry about being rejected, disliked, or seen as greedy. So they say nothing, accept terms as-is, and walk away underpaid.

But what they don't realize is that silence IS a negotiation. By not speaking, you've agreed to whatever deal is offered. Every "okay" without pushback is you negotiating against yourself.

A Parable: The Merchant's Apples

A farmer brought apples to market. The first buyer said, "I'll give you one coin per apple." The farmer accepted quickly. Later, another farmer with the same apples said, "One coin is too little. I want three." After debate, they settled at two. Both farmers sold apples. One walked home with half the profit because he never asked. The apples weren't different. The difference was negotiation.

Case Study: The Young Artist's Chains

History is filled with artists who signed away their future for short-term crumbs. A label offers $75,000 to a struggling young rapper. That money feels life-changing in the moment. But the contract says the label owns publishing, masters, and touring rights. The artist is effectively an employee, locked out of the royalties forever. His music streams in the millions, bringing in tens of millions to the label. He sees scraps.

This isn't a rare story. It's the norm. From blues musicians in the 1930s, to soul singers in the 1960s, to rappers in the 1990s, to YouTubers signing with networks today — lack of negotiation keeps creators poor while companies feast.

Meanwhile, those who master negotiation flip the script. Look at Jay-Z. He walked into meetings with the leverage of owning his masters and refused predatory contracts. Rihanna negotiated Fenty partnerships instead of signing away ownership. These moves weren't luck. They were the result of negotiation skill.

Predictions if Unchecked

If people continue avoiding negotiation, the gap between creators and corporations will widen. Workers will keep making less than they're worth. Artists will keep signing slave deals. Everyday consumers will overpay for cars, homes, and credit. Generations will pass down silence as a "survival tactic," teaching children to accept whatever is handed to them.

In twenty years, the wealthy won't just be those with money — they'll be those who know how to negotiate. Everyone else will still be begging for fairness.

Strategies to Break the Trap

Do the Research: Know market value before any deal. Information is leverage.

Practice Counter-Offers: Even asking for more is better than silence.

Detach Emotion: Negotiation is not about feelings; it's about terms.

Role-Play Scenarios: Practice with friends, mentors, or even alone. Build muscle memory.

Start Small: Negotiate everyday things — bills, subscriptions, even food portions. Build confidence.

Know When to Walk: The ability to leave the table is ultimate leverage.

Learn the Language: Contracts have traps. Understand publishing, royalties, interest, equity.

Closing Manifesto

Life itself is negotiation. Every deal, every conversation, every exchange of value is a tug-of-war. Without negotiation skills, you're not tugging. You're being dragged.

To lack negotiation is to declare you trust strangers more than you trust yourself. It is to believe the world is fair when history proves it's not. It is to hope the lion will eat someone else when you are the one standing in front of its mouth.

Learn to negotiate, or prepare to live as a servant in a world built by sharper tongues. Because the reality is brutal but simple: in every deal, somebody eats more. If you don't negotiate, it will never be you.

Chapter 1 – Staying in the House

Most people don't realize how much a door can cost. Not the kind you buy at Home Depot. I'm talking about the invisible door between you and the world — the one you lock every day when you decide to stay inside, scrolling your life away, convincing yourself you're "safe."

But safety is expensive. Safety steals opportunity. Safety kills wealth.

The Cost of Isolation

There are two types of people in this world: those who collide with opportunity, and those who wait for it to knock. Guess what? Opportunity doesn't knock. It's out in the streets, at the networking event, in the gym, at the restaurant, on the train, at the coffee shop, in that awkward conversation you didn't want to have. You staying inside guarantees you'll miss it.

Scott Galloway was right: studies show that young people who leave the house more often, who build social capital in real-world environments, end up with higher net worths. Why? Because net worth isn't built on dollars first — it's built on networks. Every chance encounter can redirect your entire trajectory. You think Jeff Bezos met investors staying in his living room? You think Jay-Z built an empire staying on the block? No. They stepped into rooms, some hostile, some uncomfortable, but all necessary.

The house feels comfortable, but it's a coffin if you let it become your world.

Corporate POV vs. Street POV

Corporate POV: The guy who never leaves the office happy hour doesn't just drink — he gets promoted. He learns who the decision-makers are. He overhears strategy. His face becomes familiar. That familiarity turns into trust, and trust turns into opportunity. If you're at home "resting," you've already lost ground.

Street POV: The hustler who never steps off his porch never learns the lay of the land. He doesn't see who's moving weight, who's getting money, where the demand is. He doesn't hear the rumors, the risks, the shifts in power. He's blind. The man moving around the city, shaking hands, breaking bread, and learning people's rhythms? He's the one who survives raids, adapts to droughts, and builds connections that turn into empires.

Whether boardroom or block, one truth is universal: if people don't see you, they can't trust you. If they don't trust you, they don't pay you.

The Psychology of the Couch

Why do so many stay in the house? It's deeper than laziness. It's fear. Fear of rejection, fear of judgment, fear of the unknown. People convince themselves "outside is dangerous," but in reality, the bigger danger is invisibility.

The human brain is wired for connection. Studies from Harvard's longest-running research on adult development show that strong relationships are the single biggest predictor of both happiness and financial security. Isolation, on the other hand, correlates with poverty, addiction, and even early death. Staying inside isn't neutral — it's toxic.

A Parable: The Closed Window

There was once a young man who kept his window closed. He said the air outside was too dirty, too unpredictable. One day, opportunity walked down his street, knocking on doors. It skipped his house — no light, no sound, no sign of life. Years later, the man opened his window, and the world had passed him by. He realized too late: clean air had never been the goal. It was breath itself.

Case Study: The Invisible Graduate

Meet Marcus. Smart, degree in hand, talent for graphic design. But Marcus stayed in his room. He applied to jobs online, complained about no callbacks, and drowned his anxiety in Netflix binges. His classmate Jasmine wasn't as talented, but she showed up at every networking event, volunteered at conferences, posted her work publicly. Within a year, Jasmine had contracts, freelance income, and a mentor at a major firm. Marcus had depression and unpaid bills.

The difference wasn't skill. It was visibility.

Predictions if Unchecked

If the culture of staying inside continues, we're looking at a generation of ghosted potential. Whole communities will vanish from the economic playing field. Loneliness will skyrocket. AI and automation will replace workers who never built real connections. Men will retreat further into video games and online fantasies, women into filtered social media validation, while the real wealth shifts hands in face-to-face rooms they'll never enter.

In twenty years, the divide won't just be rich vs. poor. It'll be visible vs. invisible.

Strategies to Break the Trap

Set a Minimum: Leave the house at least once a day with intention. Not just for errands — for exposure.

Targeted Environments: Go where opportunity lives: gyms, libraries, networking events, upscale lounges, trade shows, even volunteering. Be strategic.

Micro-Interactions: Speak to strangers. Compliment. Ask questions. Build micro-muscles of connection. Small talk compounds.

Document Presence: Share your journey publicly. It multiplies reach. The digital world can amplify, but the real world verifies.

Accountability Partner: Have someone who checks if you've been outside making moves. Pressure makes consistency stick.

Closing Manifesto

Doors are dangerous. Not because of who can break in, but because of who you keep out. Every day you stay inside, you choose comfort over collision, invisibility over recognition, stagnation over growth. The couch is the coffin of ambition.

Step outside. Breathe the air of discomfort. Shake hands that feel awkward. Enter rooms that feel above you. Because every opportunity you dream of is already outside — and it's walking past your house every single day.

If you stay in, you've already lost.

Chapter 2 – Being Overweight / Underweight

Money is shallow before it's deep. That's the truth most people don't want to admit. Your body — the first thing people see — often decides whether doors open or close for you. People love to say "don't judge a book by its cover," but the world runs on judgment. And the cover you walk around in is your body.

This isn't about body-shaming. This is about economics. Your body is currency, whether you choose to acknowledge it or not. Employers judge it. Clients judge it. Investors judge it. Partners judge it. Strangers judge it. And while they're judging, they're also making decisions that affect your opportunities.

The Economics of First Impressions

Research from Princeton shows that humans form an impression in less than a second of seeing someone. That impression doesn't just shape attraction — it shapes trustworthiness, competence, and even intelligence. Now, whether those impressions are accurate doesn't matter. What matters is they're happening. If you walk into a room overweight and sloppy, people unconsciously link you to laziness, lack of discipline, and unreliability. If you walk in underweight, frail, or unhealthy-looking, they unconsciously tag you as weak, fragile, or incapable.

None of that may be true. But perception doesn't care about truth. Perception creates reality.

Corporate POV vs. Street POV

Corporate POV: A hiring manager looks at two candidates. One is fit, confident, dressed clean. The other is equally skilled but looks unwell, tired, overweight, or unkempt. Subconsciously, the manager leans toward the fitter candidate. Why? They assume discipline, energy, and resilience — all traits tied to leadership. That "look" translates into promotions, raises, and opportunities.

Street POV: The hustler who looks weak gets tested. The hustler who looks sloppy gets disrespected. On the street, appearance is survival. If you're overweight, you get called slow. If you're underweight, you get called soft. Either way, people gauge how far they can push you, and money follows respect. Respect follows presence. Presence follows how you present yourself physically.

The boardroom and the block speak the same language: your body is your billboard.

The Hidden Costs of Health Neglect

Being overweight or underweight doesn't just affect perception — it affects energy, stamina, and focus. An unhealthy body drags your mind into survival mode. When you're tired, bloated, or starving, your brain chemistry changes. Studies in physiology prove that chronic fatigue lowers willpower, weakens decision-making, and increases risk-taking. That means you make worse financial choices.

Add to that the cost of medical bills, prescriptions, or low productivity. Poor health eats wealth silently from every direction.

A Parable: The Two Fighters

Two men trained for a fight. One ate well, built his strength, and showed discipline daily. The other said, "My skill will carry me," and ignored his body. On fight day, both entered the ring with equal knowledge, but one carried armor and the other carried weakness. The crowd didn't remember the techniques. They remembered who stood tall after the blows. The lesson: knowledge without a strong vessel collapses under pressure.

Case Study: The Promotion That Never Came

Jessica worked in a corporate office. Smart, skilled, always met deadlines. But she struggled with her weight and presentation. Colleagues respected her work, but leadership overlooked her for promotions. Meanwhile, a less skilled but fitter coworker rose quickly. Years later, Jessica learned the truth in a casual conversation: her superiors questioned her "energy and discipline" simply by how she looked walking into meetings. They equated her body with her professional potential. She was robbed of opportunities not because of her mind, but because of her vessel.

On the flip side, look at athletes-turned-businessmen. Magic Johnson, Shaq, Serena Williams. Their physical discipline carried into perception of leadership, opening doors beyond sports. Fitness became synonymous with power, making people trust them with billions.

Predictions if Unchecked

If this culture of neglect continues, entire communities will lose wealth before they even get a chance to make it. Poor diet and inactivity will lead to chronic disease, raising healthcare costs and draining generational savings. Employers will subconsciously gatekeep opportunities from people who don't "look the part." On the streets, unhealthy bodies will continue to invite disrespect and danger. The divide will widen: those who master their physical presence will be trusted with wealth, while those who don't will stay invisible, broke, or dependent.

In twenty years, the wealthiest communities will be the fittest ones. Not because money buys health — but because health protects money.

Strategies to Break the Trap

Health as Currency: Treat your body like an investment portfolio. Sleep, nutrition, exercise, and hygiene are non-negotiables.

Daily Movement: 30 minutes of exercise isn't optional. It compounds energy and confidence.

Nutritional Discipline: Cut cheap, addictive foods. They look affordable but bankrupt you later through health bills and lost stamina.

Accountability: Train with others. Join gyms, teams, or communities that make fitness normal.

Image Audit: Check how your physical presence lands in photos and mirrors. Adjust until your body tells the story of discipline.

Closing Manifesto

Your body is your first business card. Before you speak, before you hustle, before you create — your body speaks for you. Every pound of neglect, every ounce of weakness, every signal of indiscipline is a silent wealth killer.

No one has to like this truth, but no one can escape it. Health is economics. Energy is currency. Presence is power. If you refuse to master your body, you've already surrendered your wealth.

Take control of your vessel. Stand tall. Move with discipline. Build a body that commands respect before your mouth ever opens. Because in this world, the first impression is often the last chance.

Chapter 3 – Your Closest 5 Relationships

Show me your five closest people, and I can predict your bank account, your mindset, and your future without seeing a single receipt. That's not spiritual talk, that's math. Proximity is contagious.

Your relationships are the soil your life grows out of. Good soil produces strong roots and fruit. Toxic soil rots seeds before they sprout. And the dangerous part? Most people don't even realize they're planted in poison until it's too late.

The Mathematics of Proximity

Studies in social science call it "the law of averages." Your income tends to mirror the average of your five closest friends. If your crew is broke, lazy, or addicted to drama, you'll drown with them — not because you want to, but because habits rub off, decisions synchronize, and standards get shared.

On the flip side, if you surround yourself with driven, disciplined, and strategic people, you're forced to rise. Their moves raise your standards by default. That's why one mastermind group can change a life faster than any self-help book.

Corporate POV vs. Street POV

Corporate POV: Look at the executive floor. Promotions don't just go to the most skilled. They go to those plugged into the right circles. If you're eating lunch with complainers, gossipers, and time-wasters, leadership already knows you're one of them. Birds of a feather. But if you're sitting with problem-solvers, innovators, and deal-makers, people assume you're cut from the same cloth. That assumption becomes opportunity.

Street POV: A hustler linked with reckless friends inherits their problems. If your crew is sloppy, loud, or undisciplined, cops, rivals, and chaos come for all of you. Guilt by association is real. On the other hand, a tight crew of strategic thinkers, each playing their role, multiplies opportunity. A disciplined circle moves like a company — each skill complementing the other, each man sharpening the other.

Whether boardroom or block, your five closest people are either ladders or anchors.

The Psychology of Influence

Humans are wired for imitation. Neurological studies show we mirror the behaviors of those closest to us, even unconsciously. If your circle normalizes overspending, disrespect, or mediocrity, you adopt it as "just how life is." That mental prison is deadly.

Think about your circle. Do they talk about ideas, or do they only gossip about people? Do they strategize about investments, or do they just argue about sports? Do they celebrate your growth, or do they get quiet when you level up? The answers reveal your future.

A Parable: The Rotten Apple Basket

A farmer placed one rotten apple in a basket of fresh ones. Within weeks, the rot spread, infecting every apple. The farmer realized too late that freshness never rubs off. Decay always spreads faster.

Your circle works the same way. One toxic friend can poison the whole crew. Don't fool yourself — you are not strong enough to resist forever.

Case Study: The Unseen Chain

Malcolm was talented, ambitious, and wanted to start his own business. But his circle was stuck in high school mode — drinking every weekend, arguing over old beef, clowning anyone trying something new. Every time Malcolm shared an idea, his friends laughed it off. Over time, he stopped talking about his dreams, then stopped chasing them altogether. Ten years later, Malcolm realized he was still in the same apartment, same job, same habits. The dream had died, not because of his lack of talent, but because of his circle's lack of vision.

Contrast that with Vanessa. She joined a local entrepreneur group, started attending meetups, and made friends with people building real businesses. Within three years, she quit her job, launched a brand, and built her income higher than she imagined. Her five closest people weren't just friends — they were fuel.

Predictions if Unchecked

If people keep ignoring the power of proximity, the cycle of stagnation will continue. Entire communities will normalize mediocrity. Talented individuals will suffocate in circles that don't believe in growth. The wealthy will keep pulling ahead, not because they're smarter, but because they cluster in environments where success is the norm.

In twenty years, the wealth gap won't just be about money. It'll be about mindset — and mindset is contagious. The poor will keep babysitting each other's excuses, while the rich will keep multiplying each other's strategies.

Strategies to Break the Trap

Audit Your Circle: Write down your five closest people. Ask: Do they drain me or develop me? Do they inspire me or limit me?

Upgrade Environments: Put yourself where growth-minded people gather — conferences, workshops, gyms, libraries, mastermind groups.

Create Distance: You don't always have to cut people off immediately. Start by creating space. Limit exposure to toxic habits.

Find Accountability Partners: One person with discipline can shift your whole trajectory. Build alliances intentionally.

Be the Value: Don't just seek better people — become better yourself. High-value circles attract high-value individuals.

Closing Manifesto

You are not as independent as you think. Your five closest people are sculpting your future behind your back, brick by brick, habit by habit. Every laugh, every complaint, every conversation is writing the script of your financial destiny.

If your circle is small-minded, broke, or bitter, you are volunteering to inherit their ceiling. If your circle is disciplined, wealthy in mindset, and hungry, you are volunteering to inherit their sky.

Choose carefully. Your future is already sitting at your dinner table.

Chapter 4 – Places You Shop At and Eat At

Where you spend your money is where you spend your time, and where you spend your time decides who you collide with. Most people think shopping and eating are just about survival or taste. They miss the deeper truth: every environment you enter is a network. Every store, restaurant, or bar is a filter that sorts you into a class, a mindset, a circle of opportunity — or lack of it.

The places you shop and eat don't just feed your stomach or fill your closet. They shape your exposure, your relationships, and your chances at wealth.

The Economics of Environment

If you shop in low-quality places, you meet low-quality networks. If you eat in cheap spots where nobody's planning their future, you inherit their ceiling. Environments are contagious. Walk into a Whole Foods, and you're surrounded by health-conscious professionals. Walk into a luxury boutique, and you're bumping shoulders with people who understand status and leverage. Walk into a corner store every day, and you're breathing in mediocrity, gossip, and survival mode energy.

This isn't about being bougie. It's about positioning. If you want better, you have to place yourself where better moves.

Corporate POV vs. Street POV

Corporate POV: Executives know the best deals don't happen in boardrooms. They happen at golf courses, upscale steakhouses, charity galas, and coffee shops near financial districts. Those environments attract money, and money attracts money. A junior employee who "just happens" to be at the same café as the VP every morning will eventually strike a conversation. That conversation could change their career.

Street POV: Hustlers know territory is everything. Where you post up says everything about your level. If you're always at the gas station with dudes wasting time, you're not just wasting gas — you're wasting years. But if you hang around studios, gyms, or places where movers are, your hustle naturally upgrades. Position is power, and your stomping ground becomes your ceiling.

Whether in a suit or in sneakers, the rule is the same: the environment decides the energy.

The Psychology of Positioning

Humans are tribal. We trust people who share our spaces. If someone sees you repeatedly at a high-level restaurant, gym, or bookstore, they assume you're cut from the same cloth. That assumption leads to conversations, which lead to opportunities. This is exposure therapy for wealth. You don't belong until people see you consistently in the same environments as them.

And the reverse is true. If your daily hangouts scream poverty, recklessness, or stagnation, people of power assume you're part of that. They don't separate you from your environment.

A Parable: The Two Markets

Two merchants sold the same product. One set up his stall in a rundown market, where customers argued over pennies. The other set up in a thriving market, where customers valued quality and paid without question. Within months, the first merchant quit in frustration. The second doubled his wealth. Both had equal skill. The difference was location.

Case Study: The Lunch Table Divide

Andre worked at a tech company. Every day he ate lunch at the cheapest spot near the office, surrounded by coworkers complaining about management. Across the street, executives ate at a pricier restaurant, laughing over wine and discussing strategy. Andre never crossed that street. He never heard the conversations that shaped the company's future. Meanwhile, another junior employee started eating there occasionally, just to be in the room. Within a year, that employee was promoted — not because of skill, but because of familiarity.

On the block, the same truth plays out. The guy always in the liquor store parking lot is invisible to opportunity. The guy who spends his time in gyms, barber shops, or businesses eventually meets people who can change his life.

Predictions if Unchecked

If people keep treating shopping and eating as neutral, they'll stay boxed in by invisible ceilings. Generations will normalize cheap environments that reinforce scarcity mindsets. The wealthy will keep expanding their networks in upscale environments, while the poor will keep reinforcing each other's mediocrity in low-value hangouts.

In twenty years, the gap won't just be wealth — it'll be exposure. Some people will have lived entire lives without ever entering spaces where opportunity circulates.

Strategies to Break the Trap

Audit Your Spots: Write down where you shop and eat weekly. Do these environments connect you to growth or stagnation?

Upgrade Gradually: You don't have to live in luxury to touch it. Start with one meal a week in a higher-end environment. Observe, learn, adapt.

Mix Up Habits: Don't always go where it's cheap or convenient. Position yourself in spaces where ambition breathes.

Invest in Presence: Treat an expensive coffee or meal as a networking fee. The environment is worth more than the drink.

Strategic Familiarity: Go consistently. Familiar faces build trust, even before words are exchanged.

Closing Manifesto

Your life will rise or fall to the level of the rooms you enter. If you only shop where survival lives, survival will be your destiny. If you only eat where people waste time, wasted years will be your inheritance.

Stop confusing cheap with smart. Cheap often costs the most in the long run. Pay for positioning. Pay for exposure. Pay for rooms where your future self already lives.

Because every dollar you spend is also buying you a network. Make sure the receipt is worth it.

Chapter 5 – Poor Communication Skills

Closed mouths don't get fed. And even when the mouth opens, if it stutters, rambles, or confuses, the food still goes to someone else's plate. Communication is currency. Every contract, every sale, every deal, every introduction — it all depends on how well you can put your thoughts into words. Yet, poor communication is one of the most overlooked killers of financial potential.

The Cost of Miscommunication

Think about the number of times someone with less skill but more mouthpiece got chosen over someone better. The artist who couldn't explain his vision lost the investor. The employee who couldn't articulate her value never got the raise. The hustler who couldn't pitch his product got ignored. In a world flooded with talent, it's not always the best who win. It's the clearest.

Poor communication closes doors before they even open. It makes you invisible in rooms you fought hard to enter. Worse, it makes people underestimate you, pigeonhole you, or dismiss you altogether.

Corporate POV vs. Street POV

Corporate POV: Meetings aren't just about ideas. They're auditions. The person who speaks clearly, confidently, and concisely looks like a leader. They may not even be the smartest in the room, but they sound like someone who should be trusted. Meanwhile, the quiet genius in the corner goes unnoticed. Corporations reward clarity more than brilliance.

Street POV: On the block, respect comes from how you talk. A hustler who can't defend himself verbally gets walked over. A hustler who can't negotiate gets robbed. A hustler who can't persuade customers never moves product. Mouthpiece is survival. Whether negotiating territory or calming down a hot-headed rival, words save lives and make money.

From boardroom to block, the rule is the same: if you can't articulate your value, the world assumes you don't have any.

The Psychology of the Tongue

The brain is a machine of perception. People don't just hear your words — they hear your confidence, your clarity, your conviction. Psychological studies show that audiences rate speakers with fluent delivery as more intelligent, regardless of the actual content. That means someone with average ideas but sharp delivery can out-earn and out-influence a genius who mumbles.

This is why poor communication is such a silent killer. You may be brilliant, but if you can't package your brilliance, you'll starve.

A Parable: The Two Fishermen

Two fishermen cast their nets. One caught little because his net had holes. The other caught much because his net was tight. Words are nets. If your communication is full of holes — stuttering, unclear, weak — opportunity swims right through. If your words are strong and structured, you catch more than you expect.

Case Study: The Startup That Died in the Pitch

A small startup had a groundbreaking product — better than competitors, cheaper, more efficient. But when it came time to pitch to investors, the founder froze. He stumbled through jargon, rambled off-topic, and failed to answer direct questions with confidence. Investors passed. Months later, a weaker competitor with a better pitch raised millions and dominated the market. The startup closed within the year.

On the flip side, think of hip-hop. Rappers with sharp delivery, flow, and communication rise, even when their lyrics are average. Meanwhile, lyricists with deep content but poor delivery stay underground. It's not always fair, but it's real.

Predictions if Unchecked

If poor communication continues to plague communities, brilliant ideas will keep dying in silence. Generations of visionaries will stay broke, not because they lacked talent, but because they lacked the ability to translate talent into influence.

Corporations will keep elevating smooth talkers over hard workers. Streets will keep rewarding mouthpieces over muscle. The divide will widen: those who master communication will run companies, negotiate treaties, and sign billion-dollar contracts. Those who don't will keep clocking in, arguing at bars, and wondering why the world ignores them.

Strategies to Break the Trap

Study the Craft: Public speaking, storytelling, negotiation — these are skills, not gifts. Take courses, watch speeches, practice daily.

Record Yourself: Listen to your voice. Study your tone, clarity, and confidence. Fix weaknesses like filler words, mumbling, or monotone delivery.

Read More: The more words you consume, the sharper your vocabulary becomes. Vocabulary is ammunition.

Practice Small: Start with micro-interactions: ask strangers questions, compliment confidently, explain your ideas in one sentence.

Seek Feedback: Ask mentors or friends to critique how you speak. Ego hides growth.

Model Masters: Study great communicators — MLK, Malcolm X, Steve Jobs, Jay-Z, Maya Angelou. Don't copy their style, but absorb their clarity.

Closing Manifesto

The world doesn't pay for silence. It pays for clarity, conviction, and persuasion. Poor communication is a wealth killer hiding in plain sight.

Your mouth is your microphone. Your words are your contracts. Your tone is your handshake. If you don't control them, someone else will control the narrative about you.

Speak with discipline. Speak with conviction. Speak with purpose. Because in this world, you don't get what you deserve — you get what you can articulate.

Chapter 6 – Lack of Confidence

Confidence is the invisible currency that buys respect before money ever shows up. You can smell it, see it, and feel it when someone walks into a room. And the reverse is just as true — lack of confidence repels opportunity faster than bad credit.

It's not about arrogance. It's not about pretending. Confidence is the natural byproduct of alignment: when your clothes, smell, fitness, hygiene, and profession all communicate the same story. Without it, you move like a contradiction, and contradictions get ignored.

The Price of Insecurity

Think about how many deals are lost not because of incompetence, but because someone couldn't look another person in the eye. How many promotions slip away because a worker sat quiet in the back, afraid to speak? How many hustlers lost respect because their body language said "victim" before their mouth said "business"?

Confidence isn't just emotional. It's financial. Research shows confident people earn more, negotiate better, and recover quicker from setbacks. Employers associate confidence with leadership, even if the person isn't the most qualified. Meanwhile, insecurity reads as liability — a silent red flag that says, "Don't trust me with money."

Corporate POV vs. Street POV

Corporate POV: The employee who presents ideas with authority gets the green light. Even if the idea is half-baked, the confidence sells it. The quiet worker with the better plan gets overlooked. Confidence is the bridge between competence and recognition.

Street POV: The hustler who carries himself timidly gets taxed, tested, or ignored. The hustler who speaks with conviction commands respect, even if he's just starting out.

Confidence is protection. It's the armor that keeps predators guessing and opportunities approaching.

The lesson in both worlds: the money follows the man who believes in himself— or at least looks like he does.

The Psychology of Confidence

Confidence is contagious. Studies show people gravitate toward those who appear certain, even in uncertain situations. It's a survival instinct — in times of confusion, humans follow the one who looks like they know the way. That's why confidence beats accuracy in real time. People don't wait for the truth. They follow the energy.

On the flip side, insecurity is also contagious. Poor posture, weak voice, sloppy appearance — these signals bleed into the environment. People feel them and instinctively withdraw trust, often without realizing why.

The Hidden Ingredients of Confidence

Clothes: Not designer — clean, fitted, intentional. Clothes either sharpen your presence or blur it.

Smell: A fresh scent speaks before your words do. Hygiene is silent marketing.

Fitness: Discipline in the body projects discipline in the mind. Weak body language signals weak spirit.

Profession: When you know your craft, you stand firm. Lack of preparation destroys confidence at the root.

A Parable: The Two Lions

Two lions entered the same territory. One carried himself with a steady gaze, head high, steps slow but sure. The other crouched low, ears pinned back, unsure. The prey didn't run from the timid lion — they tested him. The confident lion didn't have to fight. His presence was the weapon.

Confidence is the roar that saves you from needing to prove yourself.

Case Study: The Negotiation That Shifted

A young entrepreneur walked into a meeting with investors. His pitch was solid, but nerves leaked through his body language. He spoke too fast, avoided eye contact, and his voice shook. The investors passed. Months later, he met a mentor who drilled him on posture, breathing, and voice. Same pitch, different presence. He secured $500,000 in funding. Nothing changed but his confidence.

Meanwhile, in the streets, a man nicknamed Rico gained a reputation not because of muscle, but because of his demeanor. He walked into rooms like he belonged there. He never raised his voice, never rushed his words. That calm confidence made rivals hesitate. His reputation outgrew his resources, and soon, doors opened because people assumed he was already powerful.

Predictions if Unchecked

If lack of confidence continues to plague people, entire communities will stay locked in servitude. Brilliant ideas will die in silence. Wealth will bypass those who deserve it and land with those who simply dared to look the part.

Generations will confuse humility with insecurity, mistaking timidity for virtue. Meanwhile, bold mediocrity will keep running the world. In twenty years, the divide won't just be rich and poor — it will be visible and invisible. And invisibility is death in a world where perception is profit.

Strategies to Break the Trap

Build Micro-Confidence: Start with eye contact. Then handshakes. Then speaking in groups. Stack wins daily.

Dress with Intention: You don't need designer clothes. You need clothes that fit, are clean, and tell a story of discipline.

Master Your Craft: Nothing builds confidence like preparation. Know your lane so well that doubt has no room.

Fix Your Posture: Stand tall, shoulders back. Body language speaks before your mouth does.

Smell Like Discipline: Hygiene and fragrance are silent billboards. Neglect is noticed instantly.

Practice Exposure: Confidence grows in the field, not in theory. Put yourself in uncomfortable spaces until they become normal.

Closing Manifesto

Confidence is the down payment on every opportunity you'll ever have. Without it, doors stay closed. With it, doors swing open before you even knock.

This world doesn't reward the timid. It doesn't pay the silent. It doesn't trust the shaky. Confidence is not an accessory — it's armor. It's the invisible suit you wear into every battle.

So build it. Guard it. Project it. Because in the economy of respect, confidence is the only accepted currency. And if you can't afford it, you can't afford wealth.

Chapter 7 – Blind Obedience

Obedience keeps society running. But blind obedience keeps people broke. There's a difference between discipline and slavery. Discipline builds wealth. Blind obedience kills it.

The system is designed to reward you for following orders just long enough to keep you dependent. Schools teach you to obey bells, bosses, and authority without question. Jobs teach you to clock in, sit down, stay quiet, and go home. Religions, governments, and corporations thrive off people who never ask why. But when it comes to building wealth, blind obedience is one of the most dangerous killers.

The Trap of Following Orders

Obedience feels safe. No responsibility, no risk, no accountability. Just do what you're told and survive. But wealth doesn't come from survival. Wealth comes from creation, leadership, and rebellion against the limits placed on you.

Look at history. Every major breakthrough — technological, political, or economic — came from someone who refused to obey. Steve Jobs didn't obey when he dropped out of college. Frederick Douglass didn't obey when he taught himself to read. Rosa Parks didn't obey when she refused to give up her seat. Wealth, freedom, and progress come from strategic disobedience.

Blind obedience ensures you stay a worker. Controlled. Replaceable. Disposable.

Corporate POV vs. Street POV

Corporate POV: The obedient employee follows every rule, never challenges ideas, never speaks up. He's liked, but never respected. He gets the "safe" jobs but never the promotions. Meanwhile, the employee who challenges respectfully, who proposes new solutions, who bends rules to get results — that's the one leadership notices. The company exploits the obedient but invests in the disobedient.

Street POV: On the block, blind obedience gets you killed. The follower who runs every errand, takes every order, never questions the leader? He's the most expendable. The hustler who thinks independently, who moves smart even against orders, gains respect and eventually earns leadership. Obedience without thought is weakness. Strategy with action is power.

The Psychology of Obedience

Psychology experiments prove how dangerous blind obedience is. In the Milgram study, participants were instructed to "shock" another person when they got answers wrong. Most obeyed, even when they believed they were causing serious harm, simply because authority told them to. Translate that to money: most people keep working dead-end jobs, paying predatory bills, and obeying broken systems simply because someone in power said "that's how it is."

Blind obedience numbs critical thinking. It kills curiosity. And once curiosity dies, wealth potential dies with it.

A Parable: The Chained Elephant

As a baby, an elephant is chained to a post. It tries to break free but fails. After enough failures, it gives up. Even when grown — strong enough to break the chain with ease — it never tries again. The chain isn't on its leg anymore. It's on its mind.

That's blind obedience.

Case Study: The Worker Who Never Questioned

David worked for the same company for 25 years. He never challenged management, never asked for more money, never pushed for better positions. He thought loyalty would be rewarded. When the company downsized, David was laid off with nothing but a handshake. No pension, no backup plan, no wealth. His obedience was his downfall.

Meanwhile, another employee at the same company constantly questioned processes, suggested improvements, and networked with leadership. She eventually left, started her own consulting firm, and charged the same company triple for the same work she used to do as an employee. The difference wasn't skill. It was obedience.

Predictions if Unchecked

If blind obedience continues to dominate, whole generations will stay trapped as permanent workers. Corporations will keep milking loyalty until people burn out. Communities will stay dependent on systems designed to exploit them. And innovation will suffocate under the weight of "don't rock the boat."

In twenty years, the wealth gap won't just be about resources. It'll be about thinking. The obedient will still be clocking in. The strategic rebels will own the clocks.

Strategies to Break the Trap

Question Authority: Don't accept "that's how it's always been." Ask why.

Practice Strategic Disobedience: Break rules that keep you stagnant, but with strategy, not recklessness.

Build Independent Streams: Don't depend on one system for survival. Multiple incomes weaken the chains of obedience.

Study Systems: Learn how laws, banks, jobs, and schools really work. Knowledge turns orders into options.

Lead Yourself: Set your own rules. Discipline yourself so no one else has to.

Closing Manifesto

Obedience without thought is slavery with a smile. Wealth doesn't belong to the obedient. It belongs to the thinkers, the challengers, the ones who refuse to accept cages disguised as careers.

Question everything. Challenge respectfully. Break strategically. Obey only when it serves your freedom. Because if you live your life by orders, don't be surprised when your wealth belongs to the one giving them.

Chapter 8 – Limitless Loyalty

Loyalty is a noble word, but when it has no boundaries, it becomes a leash. What people call "loyalty" is often just manipulation disguised as virtue. Companies, friends, lovers, even families will demand endless loyalty while giving crumbs in return. And while you stand tall claiming "I'm loyal," your time, energy, and future wealth are bleeding out at their feet.

Loyalty is powerful — but only when it's earned, balanced, and reciprocal. Limitless loyalty, blind loyalty, is one of the most dangerous killers of financial potential.

The Trap of Endless Giving

The world applauds loyalty because it benefits power. Employers love loyal workers because they stay underpaid without complaint. Toxic partners love loyal people because they tolerate disrespect without leaving. Governments love loyal citizens because they keep paying into broken systems without revolt.

But ask yourself: where is the loyalty back? If the company will replace you in a week, if the friend will disappear when you're broke, if the partner will betray you when temptation comes — what exactly are you protecting with your loyalty? Too often, it's just an illusion.

Loyalty with no limits is slavery.

Corporate POV vs. Street POV

Corporate POV: The loyal employee works nights, weekends, holidays. They sacrifice family, health, and personal dreams. Management praises them with words, not dollars. Then, when profits dip, they're laid off like yesterday's trash. Meanwhile, the employee who stayed loyal only to their purpose — building skills, networking, side hustling — walks away with leverage. Corporations exploit loyalty. They respect independence.

Street POV: On the block, loyalty can mean life or death. But limitless loyalty often means dying for someone else's mistake. Many soldiers stayed loyal to leaders who wouldn't even send bail money when they got locked up. The hustler who learns to balance loyalty with self-preservation survives. The one who confuses loyalty with being a doormat ends up in a casket or forgotten.

The boardroom and the block are mirrors: loyalty is respected, but only when it's mutual and bounded.

The Psychology of Loyalty

Psychologically, humans crave belonging. Loyalty feels safe because it means you're part of something bigger than yourself. But that craving gets exploited. Manipulators know that once you label yourself "loyal," you'll tolerate anything to avoid the shame of betrayal. This is how entire communities stay stuck — too loyal to dead-end jobs, too loyal to failing traditions, too loyal to toxic people.

The brain convinces you that leaving means dishonor. In reality, leaving often means survival.

A Parable: The Burning House

A man stood inside a burning house. His friend outside yelled, "Come out!" But the man replied, "I can't — this house raised me. I must stay loyal." Minutes later, the house collapsed. His loyalty killed him. The lesson? Loyalty to destruction is suicide.

Case Study: The Employee Who Gave Too Much

Carla worked at a retail chain for 18 years. She never missed a day, covered shifts for everyone, and lived by the word "loyal." When the company restructured, she was fired with no severance. Meanwhile, another worker who jumped companies every 3–4 years had higher pay, better benefits, and more freedom. Carla's loyalty became her trap.

In the streets, a man named Dre stayed loyal to his crew even when their moves got sloppy. One night, he went down with them in a raid. While they negotiated deals to save themselves, Dre got the harshest sentence. His loyalty wasn't honored — it was exploited.

Predictions if Unchecked

If limitless loyalty continues, more people will waste their prime years tied to people and systems that will never repay them. Generations will keep pouring loyalty into jobs that vanish, relationships that drain, and leaders that betray. Communities will remain trapped in cycles of misplaced faith, while those who balance loyalty with strategy will own the future.

In twenty years, the divide will be clear: some will inherit freedom because they learned to redirect loyalty toward vision. Others will inherit bitterness because they stayed loyal to cages.

Strategies to Break the Trap

Redefine Loyalty: Loyalty should be to principles and purpose, not just people or companies.

Set Boundaries: Ask, "At what point does this loyalty cost me more than it gives?" Draw that line and enforce it.

Test Reciprocity: If they can't show up for you the way you show up for them, their loyalty card is revoked.

Prioritize Self-Loyalty: Be loyal to your health, your time, your dreams. Everything else comes second.

Exit with Dignity: Walking away isn't betrayal when staying means destruction.

Closing Manifesto

Loyalty without limits is not love. It is a contract of exploitation. Companies, crews, and people will drain you dry if you let them.

Be loyal to truth, to growth, to vision, to self-respect. Anything else is a slow suicide. Limitless loyalty doesn't make you noble. It makes you disposable.

So guard your loyalty like treasure. Spend it wisely. Protect it with boundaries. Because the richest people aren't the most loyal — they're the most strategic about who and what they give themselves to.

Chapter 9 – Lack of Equipment

Money without tools is like water in a broken cup. No matter how much you pour in, it leaks out. Most people never realize that the equipment they own — or don't own — directly decides their earning ceiling.

This isn't about being rich. It's about being prepared. A man can work the hardest job in the world, but if all his money goes into bills and pleasures while his house lacks the basic tools to generate income, he's still one pink slip away from poverty. A woman can have six-figure skills, but if she never invests in the equipment to sell, record, or create independently, she's chained to her employer forever.

Lack of equipment is a silent wealth killer.

The Economics of Tools

Throughout history, tools created empires. The plow turned farmers into landowners. The printing press turned words into wealth. The laptop turned bedrooms into boardrooms. Those who owned the tools had leverage. Those who didn't stayed workers.

Today, the same rule applies. A mechanic with his own shop tools sets his own prices. A videographer with cameras and editing software can start a business tomorrow. But a man with no equipment, no matter how much hustle, has to beg for permission to eat.

Corporate POV vs. Street POV

Corporate POV: The employee who relies solely on company equipment stays chained. The one who buys their own laptop, software, or tools on the side can freelance, consult, and pivot when layoffs hit. Corporate life favors the self-equipped.

Street POV: A hustler with no equipment is a liability. If you sell food with no grill, you're begging for space in someone else's kitchen. If you cut hair with no clippers, you're begging for favors. Hustlers with tools don't beg. They move. Equipment is independence.

The rule is universal: no equipment, no leverage.

The Psychology of Ownership

There's a shift in your mind when you own your own tools. It's the difference between asking and deciding. Ownership produces confidence. Borrowing produces dependency. That dependency leaks into your spirit, making you hesitant, apologetic, less bold.

But when you have your own setup — whether it's a home office, a camera kit, a food truck, or a toolbox — your brain knows: "I can create income without asking anyone." That mindset is wealth itself.

A Parable: The Two Builders

Two builders were hired to construct houses. One owned his own hammer and saw. The other borrowed from the foreman. When payday came, the one with tools was able to start his own projects, building wealth on the side. The other waited weeks for another job. Same skill, different destiny. The difference was equipment.

Case Study: The Laid-Off Coder

Daniel was a software engineer making six figures. When layoffs hit, his coworkers panicked. Daniel had already invested in a powerful home computer setup, coding software, and online courses. Within weeks, he was freelancing, building apps, and consulting. His equipment turned unemployment into independence.

On the other hand, Tasha worked at a hair salon but never bought her own chair, clippers, or dryer. When the shop closed, she was stuck. Years of talent meant nothing because she had no equipment. She had to start from scratch, broke and bitter.

Predictions if Unchecked

If people keep neglecting equipment, generations will stay chained to jobs and systems that can replace them at any time. Communities will keep hustling with raw skill but no leverage, always asking permission to survive. And corporations will keep milking this dependency, offering just enough tools to keep workers obedient but never free.

In twenty years, the divide will be sharp: those with equipment will own small empires. Those without will still beg for shifts, clients, or favors.

Strategies to Break the Trap

Invest Early: Before you buy luxuries, buy tools. Every purchase should answer: “Can this make me money?”

Start Small: Don’t wait for perfection. A cheap camera, a used laptop, a starter kit — grow as you go.

Build a Home Setup: Whether it’s a desk, a garage workspace, or a studio corner, create a space where money can be generated.

Diversify Equipment: Tools for one skill are good. Tools for multiple skills are wealth. Stack them.

Protect Your Gear: Equipment is capital. Maintain, insure, and respect it like cash.

Closing Manifesto

A worker with no tools is a servant. A hustler with no equipment is a beggar. Skills without tools are birds with clipped wings.

Invest in your equipment before you invest in your pleasures. Own the tools, own the leverage, own the freedom. Because in the war for wealth, the only soldiers who survive are the ones armed with their own gear.

No equipment, no independence. And no independence, no wealth.

Chapter 10 – Lack of Adaptation / Slow Adaptation

Adaptation is survival. Always has been, always will be. The dinosaur had size, power, and dominance — yet it's extinct. The cockroach had adaptability — and it's still here. Wealth works the same way. If you can't adapt, if you cling to old ways while the world shifts beneath your feet, you're signing your own financial death certificate.

Slow adaptation is a silent wealth killer because money moves faster than tradition, and opportunity rewards those who pivot first.

The Cost of Standing Still

The world doesn't wait for you to catch up. Technology doesn't pause because you're comfortable. Markets don't stop because you're resistant. Every day you delay adaptation, someone else takes the position you could have held.

Think about Blockbuster. They laughed at Netflix. They thought people would never give up DVDs. Today, Blockbuster is a memory, and Netflix is a giant. The difference wasn't resources. It was adaptation.

At the personal level, the same rule applies. The man who refuses to learn new skills because "he's too old" becomes obsolete. The woman who refuses to embrace new tools because “it’s not her thing” loses ground. Comfort is expensive. Resistance is bankruptcy.

Corporate POV vs. Street POV

Corporate POV: The worker who learns new systems, adapts to new markets, and embraces new strategies rises quickly. The worker who resists change becomes a liability. Companies don’t reward “I’ve always done it this way.” They fire it.

Street POV: Hustlers who refused to adapt to new ways of making money died broke. The ones who adjusted — shifting from CDs to streaming, from corner sales to online markets, from street hustles to legal businesses — survived. Adaptation is the difference between being a legend or a cautionary tale.

The Psychology of Resistance

Psychologists call it “status quo bias.” Humans cling to what’s familiar, even when it’s killing them. We fear the unknown more than we fear the guaranteed pain of staying stuck. That’s why so many people stay in dead-end jobs, toxic relationships, or outdated mindsets. They’d rather die comfortable than live uncertain.

But here’s the truth: uncertainty is where money lives. Every new trend, every new market, every new invention starts as uncertain. Those who adapt first eat first.

A Parable: The Rigid Tree

A storm hit the forest. The rigid oak tree stood tall, refusing to bend. The flexible bamboo bent with the wind, swayed, and survived. When the storm passed, the oak lay broken, while the bamboo still stood. Wealth is the same storm. Rigidity breaks you. Adaptability saves you.

Case Study: The Taxi Driver vs. The Uber Driver

For decades, taxi drivers ruled cities. When Uber arrived, many drivers laughed, refused, and cursed the app. They held onto old medallions, convinced nothing would change. Within years, their incomes collapsed. Meanwhile, early Uber adopters thrived, making more money, gaining flexibility, and owning the future of transportation. Same skill — driving. Different outcome — adaptation.

Another case: Samira, a seamstress. While her peers stuck to physical shops, she learned to market her work online, built an Instagram presence, and shipped worldwide. Within three years, she multiplied her income tenfold. The others closed their shops, still waiting for foot traffic.

Predictions if Unchecked

If people keep resisting adaptation, whole communities will fall behind. Jobs will vanish. Skills will expire. Wealth will bypass those who cling to old ways. The divide won't just be between rich and poor. It'll be between fast and slow.

In twenty years, the world won't just reward intelligence. It will reward speed. The first to learn, pivot, and adapt will inherit opportunity. The last will inherit excuses.

Strategies to Break the Trap

Kill Ego: Admit when your way no longer works. Pride is the enemy of adaptation.

Learn Relentlessly: Take courses, read, watch, experiment. Make learning a lifestyle.

Embrace Technology: Don't fear new tools. Master them. Early adoption is leverage.

Test Quickly: Don't wait for perfect conditions. Try, fail, pivot, repeat.

Stay Curious: Curiosity is the fuel of adaptation. When curiosity dies, so does relevance.

Closing Manifesto

The world doesn't slow down for your comfort. The storm of change is constant. Those who bend survive. Those who resist break.

Adaptation is not optional. It is oxygen. Refuse it, and you choke. Embrace it, and you breathe wealth.

Your survival, your relevance, your future net worth depend on how quickly you adjust to what's new. Be the first to bend, not the last to break.

Chapter 11 – No Planning / Poor Strategy

Life without a plan is like playing chess blindfolded. You don't see the board, you don't see the pieces, and you wonder why you keep losing. Most people aren't broke because they don't work hard. They're broke because they don't have a plan. And the few who do? Their plans are weak, short-term, or built on illusions.

No planning and poor strategy are wealth killers because they turn ambition into chaos and time into wasted motion.

The Illusion of "Figuring It Out Later"

People love to say, "I'll figure it out as I go." That mindset works for vacations, not for financial survival. Money rewards precision. Strategy turns years into decades of advantage. Lack of planning leaves you vulnerable to every storm: layoffs, medical bills, market shifts, even small emergencies.

A man with no plan spends every dollar he earns. A man with a poor plan invests in get-rich-quick schemes, chases trends, and plays checkers on a chessboard. Both end up in the same place: broke and confused.

Corporate POV vs. Street POV

Corporate POV: Companies that plan thrive. They project revenue, study markets, and build long-term strategies. Employees who don't plan their careers stagnate. The one who maps out skills, promotions, and networks climbs. The one who drifts gets replaced.

Street POV: Hustlers without strategy get caught slipping. No lookout, no backup, no escape plan. Hustlers with strategy run crews like companies. They calculate risk, diversify income, and prepare for droughts. One lives. The other ends up locked up or laid out.

Both sides prove the same law: lack of planning is suicide.

The Psychology of Short-Sightedness

The brain loves instant gratification. That's why most people plan for Friday night, not for the next five years. Psychologists call it "temporal discounting" — we undervalue the future compared to the present. That's why someone will spend $500 on shoes today instead of investing $500 in tools or stocks that could grow. It feels better now, but it kills the future.

The wealthy override this instinct. They plan, delay gratification, and trade today's comfort for tomorrow's freedom. The poor indulge, improvise, and stay trapped.

A Parable: The Two Farmers

Two farmers planted seeds. One scattered randomly, hoping for luck. The other mapped his rows, studied the soil, and timed the seasons. When harvest came, the first had weeds and scraps. The second had abundance. Both worked, but only one planned.

Case Study: The Business That Collapsed

Jerome started a clothing brand. He had talent, designs, and ambition. But no plan. No inventory strategy, no marketing calendar, no budgeting. He lived by the motto "we'll figure it out." At first, sales came in. But when demand grew, he couldn't fulfill orders. When competition rose, he had no response. Within a year, the brand died.

Contrast that with Keisha, who started smaller but with a strategy. She projected costs, tracked trends, built systems. Five years later, her brand expanded into multiple states. The difference wasn't skill — it was planning.

Predictions if Unchecked

If poor strategy continues, generations will keep running in circles — working harder but never smarter. Communities will celebrate hustling but never structure. The talented will die broke while the strategic multiply wealth.

In twenty years, the wealth gap will not just be about resources but about foresight. The planners will own companies, land, and time. The improvisers will still be borrowing money for rent.

Strategies to Break the Trap

Write It Down: A plan in your head is a wish. On paper, it becomes a roadmap.

Set Horizons: Plan in layers — daily, monthly, yearly, decade. Build short-term moves that serve long-term goals.

Study Patterns: History repeats. Learn from markets, mentors, and mistakes.

Prepare for Storms: Build emergency funds, backup skills, and alternate routes. Strategy isn't just growth — it's defense.

Review & Adapt: A plan that never evolves dies. Revisit regularly and refine.

Closing Manifesto

Effort without strategy is wasted breath. Money without planning is water through a sieve. The world doesn't reward the hardest worker. It rewards the smartest planner.

If you want wealth, stop drifting. Map your life like it's a battlefield, because it is. Every dollar is a soldier. Every hour is a weapon. Deploy them with precision, or lose them in chaos.

No plan, no future. Poor strategy, poor life. Choose carefully.

Chapter 12 – Inner Child Syndrome

The body grows, but the mind often doesn't. Too many adults walk around in grown frames while their decision-making is still frozen in high school. That's Inner Child Syndrome — the unhealed child inside dictating your money moves, your relationships, your habits, and ultimately, your wealth.

It's not always visible. It's not just about immaturity. It's about unresolved wounds, lack of guidance, and emotional stunting that quietly sabotages financial growth. Inner Child Syndrome is one of the most overlooked wealth killers because it disguises itself as personality. People say, "That's just who I am." No — that's who your unhealed child is.

The Cost of Living Like a Teenager

Adults trapped in Inner Child Syndrome prioritize validation over vision. They chase trends, not strategy. They seek approval, not independence. They avoid responsibility because it feels too heavy, so they indulge in distractions — parties, gossip, overspending — while years slip away.

Financially, it shows up as:

Buying status symbols to impress peers, like a teenager craving clout.

Running from discipline because "it feels boring."

Blowing money on short-term pleasures instead of long-term investments.

Avoiding tough conversations about money, credit, or legacy because it feels uncomfortable.

The result? Adults with teenage spending habits and childlike emotions are destined for lifelong financial struggle.

Corporate POV vs. Street POV

Corporate POV: Inner Child Syndrome shows up in employees who crave validation from bosses. They overwork for applause but never negotiate pay. They want to be "liked," so they avoid conflict, letting others eat off their plate. They confuse loyalty with servitude because they're still trying to impress authority figures like parents they never satisfied.

Street POV: On the block, the inner child fuels reckless hustles. Quick money, flashy purchases, and loud reputations scream insecurity. Grown men still beefing over respect like teenagers in a lunchroom. Hustlers dying over Instagram comments instead of moving smart. That childish mindset kills more futures than bullets.

In both worlds, the child inside refuses to grow up — and money pays the price.

The Psychology of the Wounded Child

Trauma freezes time. A boy abandoned at 12 may keep chasing validation at 30. A girl shamed at 15 may keep people-pleasing at 40. The unhealed child shows up in spending, saving, and decision-making. Psychologists note that unresolved childhood wounds often resurface during stress, making adults regress to childish behavior right when adult discipline is needed most.

This is why many people sabotage promotions, blow lump sums, or ruin relationships. The adult is in the room, but the child is at the wheel.

A Parable: The Empty Chair

A man hosted a dinner for success. He invited discipline, strategy, and wealth. But at the table sat an empty chair. It was reserved for the child inside him — and every time he tried to make a decision, that child whispered, "Don't grow. Stay safe. Stay fun. Stay the same." The man never ate. His feast rotted. All because he gave the child a permanent seat.

Case Study: Lottery Winners and Childhood Wounds

Most lottery winners go broke within five years. Why? Because their inner child takes control. They buy toys, chase validation, give endlessly to peers, and avoid planning. Without healing, money magnifies immaturity.

On the flip side, consider entrepreneurs who healed early. Jay-Z often speaks of leaving childish things behind to focus on legacy. That shift from chasing validation to building structure turned a hustler into a billionaire.

Predictions if Unchecked

If Inner Child Syndrome continues unchecked, generations will remain stuck in cycles of adolescent decision-making. Communities will glorify childishness — constant parties, drama, reckless spending — while other groups build empires quietly. Adults will die with teenager habits, never passing wealth because they never left high school mentally.

In twenty years, the richest divide won't be just money. It'll be maturity. Those who grew up inside will build. Those who stayed children will consume until death.

Strategies to Break the Trap

Face the Child: Identify what age your wounds froze at. Journal. Reflect. Therapy if needed. Name the child.

Build Adult Rituals: Discipline your body and mind. Wake up early. Budget. Save. Invest. Adult habits choke childish impulses.

Kill the Need for Applause: Validation is expensive. Stop buying respect. Earn it through consistency.

Practice Responsibility: Volunteer for hard tasks. Handle bills head-on. Lean into discomfort until it feels normal.

Separate Fun from Finance: Have fun, but never at the expense of your future. Pleasure without planning is poison.

Closing Manifesto

The child inside you doesn't have to die — but it cannot lead. Play belongs in your spirit. Discipline belongs in your decisions.

If you don't heal your inner child, it will keep you broke, bitter, and blind. Wealth requires adulthood. Responsibility is freedom.

Grow up, or stay stuck. The choice is yours.

Chapter 13 – Digital Identity & Algorithmic Control

You are not just who you say you are. You are who the algorithm says you are.

Every search you make, every click, every post, every like — it all builds a profile. That profile decides what ads you see, what jobs you're offered, what loans you qualify for, and sometimes even what neighborhoods you're “allowed” to live in. And the scary part? Most people have no idea this invisible identity even exists.

Your digital identity is your second skin. If you don’t control it, someone else will.

The Economics of Data

Data is the new oil. Corporations and governments mine it, refine it, and sell it for billions. You don’t even own your own shadow online — Facebook, Google, Amazon, banks, credit bureaus, they all own slices of it. And every slice adds up to a version of “you” that determines your financial trajectory.

Click too many debt relief ads? The algorithm decides you’re broke, and suddenly you see more predatory loans than wealth-building opportunities. Watch too many party videos? The algorithm decides you’re unserious, and your feed never shows investment opportunities. Apply for a job? AI systems filter you out before a human ever reads your name.

This isn’t paranoia. This is modern economics.

Corporate POV vs. Street POV

Corporate POV: Companies don’t just look at résumés anymore. They scrape social media, study digital footprints, and analyze credit histories. One sloppy tweet or reckless post can cost a career. Meanwhile, a curated online presence can open doors without you ever applying. Your digital body language is judged harder than your real one.

Street POV: Hustlers who don't understand digital identity get trapped in surveillance. Post too much, brag too loud, show every move online? You invite predators, both criminal and governmental. Smart hustlers go ghost or curate carefully. The reckless ones make the algorithm their informant.

Both sides prove the same truth: what you post, what you click, what you consume — it all decides how the system treats you.

The Psychology of the Algorithm

The algorithm isn't neutral. It learns your weaknesses and exploits them. Psychologists call it "predictive behavior modeling." Apps study how long you linger, what spikes your dopamine, what keeps you scrolling. Then they feed you more of it — even if it destroys you.

Spend too much time watching drama, and the algorithm keeps you in drama. Spend too much time on cheap entertainment, and the algorithm hides wealth-building content from you. Your digital identity becomes a mirror of your lowest habits. And then it becomes your cage.

A Parable: The Puppet Strings

A man thought he was free because he could choose what to watch. He didn't realize every choice was being tracked, measured, and fed back to him. Over time, his "choices" weren't choices anymore. They were predictions served on a silver platter. By the time he noticed the strings, the puppet master didn't need to pull them. The man danced on his own.

Case Study: The Job Candidate That Didn't Exist

Maria applied for a management position. On paper, she was perfect. But the company's AI system scraped her online identity and noticed years of posts about partying and complaints about jobs. The system flagged her as a "risk" and filtered her out. She never even got an interview.

Meanwhile, Jordan curated his digital presence. He posted industry insights, volunteered highlights, and professional milestones. Recruiters reached out to him without him applying. His digital identity made him visible and desirable.

In the streets, a rapper named D-Lo bragged online about his hustles, flashing money, cars, and guns. He went viral — then got indicted. The algorithm wasn't just entertaining him. It was building a case.

Predictions if Unchecked

If people keep ignoring their digital identity, the algorithm will own their financial destiny. Generations will be locked into echo chambers of distraction while wealth-building knowledge passes them by. Employers, lenders, and landlords will use invisible data points to gatekeep opportunities. The divide will widen: those who curate and control their digital identity will thrive. Those who don't will be silently disqualified before they even knew they had a chance.

In twenty years, digital reputation will matter more than résumés. Credit scores will merge with data scores. Social capital will be judged by algorithms that know you better than you know yourself.

Strategies to Break the Trap

Curate Your Presence: Post intentionally. Delete reckless history. Build an online persona that reflects discipline and ambition.

Control Your Consumption: The algorithm feeds what you consume. Train it by engaging with wealth-building, educational, and empowering content.

Audit Your Shadow: Google yourself. See what the world sees. Clean up anything that kills credibility.

Diversify Platforms: Don't live in one algorithm. Spread your presence and protect yourself from one system's control.

Go Ghost Strategically: Some moves should never be posted. Privacy is protection.

Closing Manifesto

Your digital identity is not a toy. It's a weapon — for or against you. The algorithm doesn't care about your dreams. It only cares about your patterns.

Control the patterns. Curate the presence. Own the story. Because if you don't, the system will write it for you — and it will write you out of wealth.

The future belongs to those who master their digital reflection. Everyone else will be owned by it.

Chapter 14 – Health & Energy Economics

Money is useless if your body is bankrupt. Wealth isn't just a bank account — it's the stamina to show up, the energy to perform, and the health to keep what you've earned. Yet most people treat their bodies like disposable machines. They grind, eat trash, sleep poorly, and then wonder why their dreams never manifest. The truth is simple: health is economics. Energy is currency. And ignoring it is one of the fastest ways to kill your wealth.

The Hidden Price of Poor Health

Every sick day is lost income. Every energy crash is a missed opportunity. Every prescription pill is money leaving your pocket forever. Chronic stress, bad diets, substance abuse, and lack of sleep don't just hurt your body — they quietly drain your financial future. Medical debt is the number one cause of bankruptcy in America. Behind almost every "financial crisis" is a health crisis ignored for too long.

But beyond bills, poor health robs productivity. A tired mind misses ideas. A sluggish body avoids risks. A foggy brain delays decisions. Money moves to those who can outlast and outperform. Without health, you're broke before the check even clears.

Corporate POV vs. Street POV

Corporate POV: Executives know energy is leverage. That's why they golf, eat clean, hire trainers, and treat health as part of business. Meanwhile, employees show up sluggish, drained, and burned out — and wonder why they're overlooked. The higher the level, the healthier the body. It's not coincidence. It's economics.

Street POV: Hustlers who party too hard, drink too much, or abuse drugs burn out early. They mistake stimulation for energy. They confuse adrenaline for stamina. The smart hustlers pace themselves, sleep enough to think straight, and treat their bodies like assets. That discipline gives them longevity. The reckless ones die young or broke.

Both sides prove one law: energy is profit.

The Psychology of Energy

Psychologists know willpower is tied to physical stamina. When your body is weak, your decisions get worse. Sleep deprivation, for example, mimics drunkenness — slow reaction times, poor judgment, impulsive choices. Diets heavy in sugar and processed food create brain fog and mood swings, making it harder to strategize or stay disciplined.

This is why health is not just about looking good. It's about thinking sharp, deciding clearly, and having the energy to follow through.

A Parable: The Broken Horse

A wealthy man owned a horse that pulled his carriage. Instead of feeding it well, he gave it scraps and beat it to move faster. The horse eventually collapsed, and the man had to walk. All his wealth couldn't move him forward anymore because he had killed his engine. The body is the horse of wealth. Treat it poorly, and your dreams collapse.

Case Study: Two Entrepreneurs

Lisa and Tony both started businesses. Lisa burned out after a year. She lived on caffeine, slept four hours a night, and ate fast food. Her body gave out, her mind crashed, and her business folded.

Tony built his health into his strategy. He worked out daily, prioritized sleep, and treated meals like fuel. When stress hit, he had the energy to push through. When competitors quit, he was still standing. Within five years, Tony's business scaled nationally. Lisa worked another job to survive.

The difference wasn't talent. It was energy economics.

Predictions if Unchecked

If health neglect continues, future generations will drown in medical debt, burnout, and short lifespans. Communities already struggling financially will compound their struggles with preventable illnesses. Employers will filter workers by energy and appearance, rewarding those who look alive and discarding the drained.

In twenty years, the wealthiest people won't just be those with money — they'll be those with stamina. The poorest will be exhausted, sedated, and permanently sick, watching life pass from hospital beds.

Strategies to Break the Trap

Treat Health as Capital: Prioritize sleep, diet, and exercise like you would investments.

Fuel, Don't Just Eat: Every meal is either fuel or poison. Choose like your money depends on it — because it does.

Master Stress: Meditation, deep breathing, or prayer aren't luxuries. They're survival tools. Stress management saves money and life.

Quit Slow Poison: Smoking, heavy drinking, drug abuse — they are delayed bankruptcy notices.

Energy Budgeting: Plan your day around peak energy times. Use prime hours for your most important work.

Closing Manifesto

Your health is your first business. Your body is your first asset. Ignore it, and you've already signed the foreclosure papers on your wealth.

Energy is currency. Stamina is profit. Discipline is insurance. Treat your body like a machine of wealth or watch it become your most expensive liability.

The truth is simple: no health, no wealth.

Chapter 15 – Relationship Capital vs. Sexual Marketplace

The relationships you choose can either multiply your wealth or bankrupt it. People underestimate how much their personal partnerships affect their financial trajectory. They think love is separate from money, but love, sex, loyalty, and partnership all have hidden price tags.

There are two currencies running at the same time: relationship capital — the networks, support, and growth you build through meaningful partnerships — and the sexual marketplace — the shallow, short-term exchanges where validation, lust, and appearance dictate value. Confuse the two, and your future collapses.

The Real Cost of the Wrong Partner

A toxic partner isn't just a headache. They are a financial liability. Arguments drain focus. Drama kills productivity. Poor spending habits multiply debt. Infidelity destroys trust and resources. An unsupportive partner clips ambition before it takes flight.

On the other hand, the right partner becomes an investor in your vision. They sharpen you, cover blind spots, and multiply your reach. One supportive relationship can change your trajectory more than ten years of grinding alone.

Corporate POV vs. Street POV

Corporate POV: Executives rise faster when they have stable partners who handle the home front, freeing them to strategize. That stability projects discipline, maturity, and trustworthiness. On the other hand, constant divorces, scandals, or messy relationships weaken reputations and cost promotions. Companies don't just invest in you. They invest in the stability you project.

Street POV: A hustler with a reckless partner gets exposed. Pillow talk leaks moves. Bad spending habits waste profits. Drama attracts heat. Meanwhile, the hustler with a loyal, strategic partner doubles his empire. She holds secrets, manages resources, and expands the hustle into a family legacy. On the block, the wrong lover can get you killed. The right one can keep you alive.

Both worlds know one truth: who you love shapes how you eat.

The Psychology of Validation

Psychologists know humans crave intimacy. But when that craving goes unhealed, people confuse validation for value. Men chase women for looks but ignore discipline. Women chase men for excitement but ignore stability. Both end up broke, heartbroken, and bitter.

This is the trap of the sexual marketplace. It rewards surface-level attraction — looks, charm, status symbols — but ignores long-term partnership value. Too many adults choose partners the way teenagers choose dates: for clout, lust, or shallow traits. Then they wonder why their bank accounts and spirits collapse.

A Parable: The Two Bridges

A man came to a river. Two bridges stood before him. One looked flashy but was made of weak wood. The other looked plain but was made of stone. The man chose the flashy bridge, and halfway across, it collapsed, drowning him. The plain bridge would have carried him safely for life. Relationships work the same way. Flash without foundation kills futures.

Case Study: The Billion-Dollar Divorce

Jeff Bezos built Amazon into a giant. His divorce cost him $38 billion. That's not gossip. That's economics. Marriage without boundaries is one of the most expensive contracts you'll ever sign. On a smaller scale, everyday divorces and breakups destroy finances. People lose homes, businesses, and years of work because they confused lust with legacy.

On the flip side, look at Barack and Michelle Obama. Whatever you think of politics, the power of that partnership is undeniable. Their combined image, discipline, and unity amplified their influence worldwide. That's relationship capital at work.

Predictions if Unchecked

If people keep chasing partners based only on sexual marketplace rules, families will keep collapsing, generational wealth will keep dissolving, and communities will stay fragmented. Toxic pairings drain more wealth than bad investments.

In twenty years, the divide will be clear: those who mastered relationship capital will pass empires to their children. Those who stayed trapped in shallow relationships will pass down nothing but stories of heartbreak and debt.

Strategies to Break the Trap

Audit Your Partner: Do they multiply or drain? Do they sharpen you or soften you? Do they invest or consume?

Choose Beyond Lust: Looks fade. Habits, mindset, and discipline endure.

Build Together: Share goals, budgets, and visions. Wealth grows faster with aligned strategy.

Protect Assets: Contracts, prenups, boundaries. Love is beautiful, but protection is smart.

Heal Before Pairing: Don't look for partners to fix wounds. Heal, then build. Broken plus broken equals broken.

Closing Manifesto

Love is not just an emotion. It's an economy. The wrong partner is bankruptcy with a smile. The right partner is compound interest in human form.

Stop letting lust decide your legacy. Stop confusing validation with value. Build partnerships that multiply discipline, peace, and vision.

Because the truth is brutal: your net worth will rise or fall to the level of the person you sleep beside.

Chapter 16 – Geography Trap

Your zip code is often more powerful than your ambition. Where you live silently dictates your opportunities, your networks, your mindset, and your exposure. Geography is not neutral — it's a filter, a gatekeeper, and for many, a trap.

People love to say, "If you've got talent, it'll shine anywhere." That's a lie. Talent buried in the wrong soil never sprouts. Geography shapes access to jobs, schools, resources, and — most importantly — people who can change your life. Staying stuck in the wrong place keeps wealth out of reach, no matter how smart, gifted, or hungry you are.

The Hidden Price of the Wrong Address

Your neighborhood decides the schools your kids go to, the banks that lend to you, the stores that serve you, and the people you bump into daily. High-crime areas scare away investment. Food deserts make health harder. Poor transit locks you out of higher-paying jobs. Even your home address on a résumé can get you filtered out before the interview.

Meanwhile, people in wealthy areas gain invisible privileges: better connections, safer environments, healthier food, faster internet, higher property values. Their geography works as a multiplier. Yours might be working as a barrier.

Corporate POV vs. Street POV

Corporate POV: Recruiters often unconsciously judge applicants by zip code. Living in an “upscale” neighborhood signals stability and professionalism. Living in a poor neighborhood can trigger bias before you even step into the room. Corporations also cluster in wealthy areas, making proximity itself an advantage.

Street POV: On the block, geography dictates survival. Hustlers stuck in certain areas can’t move without constant risk. Police presence, rival crews, and limited opportunity trap them in cycles. But the ones who learn to expand beyond their block, who travel to new spaces, meet new networks, and escape the trap — they multiply. Geography either cages or liberates you.

Both sides confirm the same rule: where you are shapes what you can access.

The Psychology of Environment

Humans absorb their environment unconsciously. Psychologists call it “environmental conditioning.” If you’re surrounded by boarded-up stores, violence, and poverty, your brain normalizes struggle. If you’re surrounded by wealth, safety, and ambition, your brain normalizes abundance. This isn't just external — it seeps into your identity.

That's why moving environments, even without money, can shift your trajectory. Exposure to better surroundings reshapes expectations. And expectations dictate decisions.

A Parable: The Caged Bird

A bird raised in a cage sang of freedom but never flew. One day, the cage door opened. The bird stayed. Why? It had confused the cage for the world. Geography had rewired its instincts.

Most people are that bird. The door is open, but fear and familiarity keep them trapped in the same geography.

Case Study: The Artist That Moved

Marcus was a talented musician stuck in a small town. His audience was limited, his network nonexistent. He finally scraped together money, moved to Atlanta, and within a year, his exposure multiplied. Same talent, different geography, new results.

Meanwhile, Tasha stayed in her hometown, working a low-paying job, waiting for opportunity to find her. Ten years later, she was still there, watching Marcus tour the world. The difference wasn't talent. It was location.

Predictions if Unchecked

If people keep ignoring the geography trap, entire communities will stay locked in cycles of poverty. Talented individuals will die in the same neighborhoods that stunted them. The wealthy will continue clustering in elite areas, compounding their advantages, while the poor normalize environments designed to limit ambition.

In twenty years, the wealth gap will look like a map. Opportunity will pool in certain regions, while other areas become economic deserts where potential goes to die.

Strategies to Break the Trap

Audit Your Geography: Ask yourself: Does my environment multiply or drain? Does it connect me to growth or keep me trapped?

Strategic Relocation: Even if temporary, moving to a place with better networks, schools, or opportunities can reset your trajectory.

Micro-Escape: If you can't move yet, spend time in higher-level environments — coffee shops, gyms, libraries, business districts. Exposure matters.

Digital Geography: The internet lets you "move" without moving. Join online spaces that connect you to higher networks.

Long-Term Plan: Treat relocation as an investment. Save, plan, and position yourself for when the opportunity comes.

Closing Manifesto

Your geography is not just an address. It's a destiny. Stay in the wrong soil, and your seeds rot. Plant yourself in richer ground, and you grow faster than you thought possible.

Stop confusing loyalty to a zip code with loyalty to your future. Love your people, but don't let the block bury your ambition.

Because the truth is clear: wealth flows where geography allows it. And if you don't move toward it, don't be surprised when it never moves toward you.

Chapter 17 – Addiction to Entertainment

Entertainment is supposed to be a break. A moment to breathe. But in today's world, entertainment isn't a break anymore — it's a trap. Screens, streams, sports, video games, social media, endless shows: people are overdosing on distraction. And that overdose costs more than time. It kills focus, productivity, and ultimately wealth.

The system is built to keep you entertained so you don't rebel. Bread and circuses — the ancient Roman strategy. Give the people food and games, and they'll ignore their chains. Fast forward to now, and the chains are Netflix binges, TikTok loops, fantasy leagues, and endless YouTube rabbit holes. Entertainment addiction is modern slavery, wrapped in 4K resolution.

The Hidden Cost of Distraction

Every hour lost to mindless entertainment is an hour stolen from building skills, strategizing, or creating income. Hours compound into months. Months compound into years. By the time people wake up, they've given a decade to watching other people live instead of living themselves.

Worse, entertainment addiction rewires the brain. It spikes dopamine, the pleasure chemical, tricking your mind into thinking you've accomplished something when all you did was scroll. This kills ambition. You feel full but you're starving.

Corporate POV vs. Street POV

Corporate POV: Executives know attention is money. That's why corporations spend billions on ads, apps, and shows engineered to keep you glued. The more entertained you are, the less you build independence. Workers addicted to shows and games come in tired, unfocused, and distracted — easy to control, easy to replace.

Street POV: Hustlers know distraction kills focus. The one glued to video games instead of perfecting the hustle falls behind. The one watching drama instead of moving product misses opportunities. On the streets, distraction isn't just unproductive — it's dangerous. If you're watching the wrong thing at the wrong time, you don't see the setup coming.

In both worlds, entertainment addiction is a weapon used against you.

The Psychology of Entertainment Addiction

Psychologists call it "variable reward loops." Apps and shows are designed like slot machines. You never know when the next laugh, shock, or thrill will come, so you keep watching. Your brain becomes hooked on unpredictability. Combine that with social validation — likes, comments, retweets — and you're trapped in an endless cycle.

Meanwhile, your real life rots. Skills decay. Energy drains. Dreams shrink. But you don't notice, because your brain is too busy getting fed fake victories.

A Parable: The Man in the Theater

A man walked into a theater to watch a play. The show was entertaining, so he stayed. Intermission came, but he refused to leave. The play continued, act after act. Years passed. When the lights finally came up, he realized his real life had been waiting outside the whole time. But the door was locked. He had traded his life for a show.

Case Study: The Wasted Decade

Anthony was obsessed with video games. Every night after work, he spent five to six hours playing. He told himself it was stress relief. Ten years later, he looked up: same job, no savings, no business, no growth. He had become an expert in virtual worlds, while the real one passed him by.

Meanwhile, Jasmine limited entertainment to one hour a day and spent the rest building her side business. Within five years, she replaced her job income. Same hours in the day, different outcomes. The difference wasn't intelligence. It was attention.

Predictions if Unchecked

If entertainment addiction continues, generations will drown in distraction while a small group of elites multiplies wealth. Communities will stay broke, not because they lack talent, but because their focus was stolen. Kids will grow up seeing more TikTok dances than financial lessons. Adults will retire with nothing but memories of shows and games that never paid a single bill.

In twenty years, the wealth divide won't just be economic — it will be attention-based. The focused will build empires. The entertained will live as spectators, clapping for lives they'll never live.

Strategies to Break the Trap

Audit Your Hours: Track how much time you spend on entertainment. Most will be shocked by the total.

Set Boundaries: Entertainment is a dessert, not a meal. One or two hours max per day, after work is done.

Replace With Creation: Every time you feel the urge to consume, ask: "Can I create instead?" Shift from spectator to producer.

Detox Regularly: Take breaks from social media, TV, or gaming. Rewire your brain to find joy in reality.

Choose Empowering Entertainment: Documentaries, educational podcasts, or biographies can entertain while fueling growth.

Closing Manifesto

Entertainment should refresh you, not own you. But too many are slaves to shows, games, and screens. They give their best hours to corporations selling ads, instead of to their own dreams.

Attention is the new currency. Protect it at all costs. Spend it on building, not bingeing. Use entertainment as seasoning, not the meal.

Because the truth is brutal: if you stay addicted to watching, you'll never be paid for doing.

Chapter 18 – Mental Health Ignored

People love to talk about money like it's separate from the mind. But every dollar you earn, every deal you make, every risk you take — it all begins in your head. Ignore your mental health, and you ignore the foundation of wealth. Anxiety, depression, trauma, and untreated stress are invisible chains. They don't just hurt your mood — they choke your earning potential.

The system thrives on this silence. Schools never teach emotional resilience. Jobs punish vulnerability. Communities shame therapy. So millions walk around broken inside, pretending they're fine, while their potential quietly bleeds out of them.

The Price of Untreated Wounds

Depression kills motivation. You stop applying, stop building, stop trying.

Anxiety kills focus. You can't think long-term when fear grips your chest.

Trauma kills trust. You sabotage relationships that could've been bridges to opportunity.

Stress kills clarity. You make reckless financial decisions just to "feel better" for the moment.

Each ignored wound is a thief. Together, they rob more wealth than any tax man.

Corporate POV vs. Street POV

Corporate POV: Workers who ignore mental health burn out, underperform, and get replaced. The corporate world now markets “wellness programs,” but most are band-aids. The truth? Companies profit more when employees suppress emotions and keep producing until they collapse. Leaders who protect their mental health outlast everyone else.

Street POV: Hustlers who ignore mental health drown in paranoia, self-sabotage, and addiction. Trauma makes them reckless. Stress leads to slips. Depression makes them freeze. The streets respect strength, but most of the recklessness we call “bravery” is untreated pain. Smart hustlers heal so they can move with clarity.

Both arenas prove the same truth: the broken mind breaks the bag.

The Psychology of Silence

Psychologists know that ignoring pain doesn’t erase it — it buries it. And buried pain resurfaces at the worst times. Childhood neglect shows up during negotiations. Past betrayals show up in marriages. Repressed anger shows up in your parenting. Suppressed grief shows up as rage in the workplace.

Ignoring mental health is like ignoring termites in your house. You don't see the damage at first, but eventually the whole structure collapses.

A Parable: The Cracked Glass

A merchant sold glasses. One cup had a small crack, invisible to the eye. Every time water was poured in, it leaked drop by drop. Over months, the crack widened, until the cup shattered in someone's hand. The merchant lost his business. One small crack destroyed the vessel because it was never repaired. That's the mind. Unrepaired cracks eventually explode.

Case Study: The Entrepreneur That Froze

Khalil launched a tech startup. On paper, he had everything: skills, investors, and vision. But he had untreated anxiety from childhood trauma. During high-pressure meetings, his hands shook, his voice cracked, and he avoided risks. Eventually, investors pulled out. His untreated mental health cost him millions.

Meanwhile, Angela, who grew up with similar trauma, invested in therapy, meditation, and journaling. She built emotional resilience. When stress hit, she navigated calmly. Her company thrived. The difference wasn't intelligence — it was mental health.

Predictions if Unchecked

If communities keep ignoring mental health, cycles of poverty will continue. Children will inherit parents' unhealed trauma. Workers will die from stress-induced diseases. Leaders will collapse under pressure, leaving legacies unfinished.

In twenty years, the wealthiest won't just be the smartest — they'll be the most emotionally resilient. Those who ignore their minds will remain stuck, no matter their skills.

Strategies to Break the Trap

Normalize Healing: Therapy, journaling, prayer, meditation — not weaknesses, but tools of wealth.

Name the Wound: You can't heal what you won't admit. Call out the depression, the anxiety, the trauma.

Build Emotional Fitness: Daily habits for the mind — gratitude practice, mindfulness, honest conversations.

Protect Mental Energy: Limit toxic people, gossip, and constant negativity. Guard your mind like your wallet.

Rest as Strategy: Sleep, silence, and recovery are weapons. The rested mind outthinks the restless.

Closing Manifesto

The unhealed mind is the poorest prison. Ignore your mental health, and you'll ignore every door wealth tries to open for you. Heal, and you unlock clarity, discipline, and resilience — the true currency of freedom.

Wealth without peace is poverty in disguise. Heal first, build next. Because if your mind collapses, everything else collapses with it.

Chapter 19 – Credit & Paperwork Literacy

The biggest scams don't happen in dark alleys. They happen on paper. Contracts, credit scores, applications, fine print — the silent assassins of wealth. Most people don't get robbed by criminals. They get robbed by clauses they never read, debts they never understood, and systems they never studied.

Credit and paperwork literacy is the hidden weapon of the wealthy. Those who master it unlock homes, loans, businesses, and leverage. Those who ignore it sign their freedom away with their own signature.

The Silent Gatekeepers

Credit determines whether you're trusted with opportunity. Paperwork determines whether you keep it. Yet schools rarely teach either. That's by design. The less you know, the easier it is to exploit you.

Bad credit inflates your costs: higher interest rates, higher insurance, even higher rent.

Poor paperwork skills lock you out of ownership: signing bad leases, agreeing to predatory loans, or getting trapped in contracts.

A lack of literacy keeps you dependent: forever renting, forever borrowing, forever asking permission.

Meanwhile, those who master the system walk into rooms with leverage. They negotiate. They own. They multiply.

Corporate POV vs. Street POV

Corporate POV: Companies thrive off paperwork ignorance. Employees sign contracts without reading, waive rights without realizing, and accept terms that bind them for decades. Corporations also reward those who do understand — people who negotiate salaries, read benefits packages, and build credit strong enough to buy homes instead of just renting forever.

Street POV: Hustlers who don't understand paperwork lose faster than they hustle. They sign record deals with predatory splits, car notes that double the value, or leases that bleed them dry. Meanwhile, the hustler who learns contracts, trademarks, and credit becomes more dangerous than any dealer — because they can own legally what others risk life for illegally.

Both sides prove the same law: ignorance of credit and paperwork guarantees poverty.

The Psychology of Avoidance

Most people fear paperwork. It looks boring, confusing, intimidating. Psychologists call this "avoidance coping" — people avoid tasks that trigger stress. But that avoidance costs thousands. Credit reports pile up with errors. Contracts get signed blind. Deadlines get missed. The wealthy lean into paperwork because they know every paragraph is either profit or prison.

A Parable: The Man Who Didn't Read

A farmer signed a contract to rent land. The paper was long, so he skipped the fine print. He worked the land for years, believing he'd one day own it. When the time came, the landlord revealed a clause: ownership was never an option. The farmer cried betrayal. The landlord shrugged. "You signed." His dream died on paper.

Case Study: The Rapper's Deal

Countless rappers sign 360 deals, handing over rights to music, touring, and merchandise. They see the upfront money, ignore the contract, and spend like kings. Years later, they're broke, while labels profit off their names forever. That's paperwork illiteracy.

On the flip side, consider Rihanna. She studied contracts, built Fenty independently, and leveraged partnerships instead of selling ownership. Her paperwork literacy made her a billionaire.

Predictions if Unchecked

If communities keep ignoring credit and paperwork, they'll stay locked out of ownership. Landlords will own their homes, banks will own their cars, and corporations will own their art. Generations will keep paying more for less, trapped in cycles of renting, borrowing, and begging.

In twenty years, the wealthiest families won't just be those with money. They'll be those who mastered paperwork — wills, trusts, contracts, credit portfolios. The poor will still be signing away futures they never read.

Strategies to Break the Trap

Study Credit: Learn how scores are built, how to repair, and how to leverage.

Read Everything: Never sign blind. If you don't understand, get help. Confusion is cheaper than regret.

Negotiate: Salaries, leases, loans — everything is negotiable if you know the terms.

Build Paperwork Systems: Keep contracts, receipts, and records organized. Order is power.

Teach the Next Generation: Make paperwork literacy a family skill. Break the cycle early.

Closing Manifesto

Paper is the battlefield of modern wealth. Every clause is a trap or a tool. Every signature is a sword or a chain.

The rich don't just make money — they master paperwork. The poor don't just lack money — they sign it away.

Stop fearing the fine print. Study it. Own it. Use it. Because if you don't master paper, paper will master you.

Chapter 20 – Reputation Economics

Money is temporary. Reputation is compound interest. In a world where information moves faster than truth, your name is your most valuable currency. Once it's ruined, doors slam shut before you even knock. Once it's solid, opportunities come looking for you without you asking.

Reputation economics is simple: your track record is your résumé, your referral, your collateral, and your shield. Ignore it, and you'll spend life trying to buy what credibility could've given you for free.

The Price of a Stained Name

One lie, one betrayal, one reckless act can erase years of work. A ruined reputation doesn't just kill relationships — it kills deals, jobs, and networks. Employers Google you. Clients ask around. Communities whisper. The world runs on trust, and reputation is trust made visible.

Meanwhile, a strong reputation pays in invisible dividends:

People recommend you without being asked.

Banks trust you with loans.

Investors feel safe betting on you.

Mentors want to help you.

Opportunities arrive already open.

A good name is an asset. A bad one is debt.

Corporate POV vs. Street POV

Corporate POV: The ambitious worker who delivers results, keeps their word, and handles pressure with integrity becomes the go-to name. Reputation earns promotions faster than résumés. Conversely, one sloppy mistake — a viral meltdown, a public scandal, a broken promise — can blacklist you permanently. Companies fire faster than they hire when reputation is at stake.

Street POV: On the block, reputation is survival. Respect is currency. A hustler with a name for loyalty and discipline can run crews without lifting a finger. But once your name is dirt — if you snitch, steal, or fold under pressure — you're finished. People don't forget, and in the streets, forgetting costs lives.

Both worlds prove the same law: reputation buys what money can't.

The Psychology of Trust

Psychologists say trust is built in drops and lost in buckets. One consistent action at a time builds credibility, but one reckless act can drain it instantly. That's why reputation must be guarded with paranoia. Your brain may forget your good deeds, but the world will never forget your failures.

A Parable: The Two Merchants

Two merchants sold gold. One built a reputation for honesty. The other mixed his gold with brass but offered discounts. At first, the dishonest merchant made more money. But when the truth came out, nobody bought from him again. The honest merchant's name spread, and his wealth multiplied. The brass merchant died broke. His greed killed his reputation.

Case Study: Warren Buffett vs. Enron

Warren Buffett famously said: "It takes 20 years to build a reputation and five minutes to ruin it." His cautious, trustworthy name has attracted investors for decades.

Contrast that with Enron, once a corporate giant. When lies and manipulation surfaced, its reputation collapsed overnight. Billions vanished. Thousands lost jobs. The brand became a synonym for betrayal.

On a smaller scale, think of local hustlers. The one who always pays debts, shows up on time, and keeps his word grows steadily. The flashy liar might rise fast, but he falls faster when his reputation catches up.

Predictions if Unchecked

If people keep ignoring reputation economics, social media will become their graveyard. One viral mistake will haunt careers forever. Communities will lose leaders to scandals that could've been avoided. The wealthy will increasingly filter partners by reputation before money. Those with no name will stay invisible. Those with ruined names will stay locked out.

In twenty years, reputation will be as measurable as credit. Digital "trust scores" will determine access. The poor won't just lack money — they'll lack credibility, which is even harder to rebuild.

Strategies to Break the Trap

Guard Your Name: Don't attach yourself to reckless people or moves. Their dirt becomes your dirt.

Keep Your Word: Reliability is rare. Every promise kept is currency in the bank.

Build Digital Discipline: What you post is forever. Protect your online trail like your financial trail.

Repair Fast: If you make a mistake, own it, fix it, and rebuild. Silence kills faster than apology.

Think Long-Term: Every action today either compounds or corrodes tomorrow's opportunities.

Closing Manifesto

Your reputation is your shadow. It walks into every room before you do. Treat it like the gold it is. Lose money, you can make it back. Lose reputation, and you may never recover.

Build a name that buys trust. Protect it like inheritance. Live so solid that your name alone opens doors your money can't.

Because the truth is timeless: wealth fades, but reputation echoes forever.

Chapter 21 – Time Mismanagement

Money is renewable. Time is not. Every dollar you lose can be replaced. Every hour you waste is gone forever. The poorest people treat time like it's infinite. The wealthiest treat it like the rarest currency. Time mismanagement is one of the deadliest silent killers of wealth because you don't notice the theft until years are gone.

Most people don't go broke from lack of money. They go broke from lack of time discipline. They waste their prime years on distractions, their peak hours on nonsense, and their golden decades on survival instead of strategy. By the time they realize, it's too late.

The Hidden Cost of Wasted Hours

Scrolling for 3 hours a day equals 45 full workdays a year.

Watching 4 hours of TV daily equals 2 months of lost productivity annually.

Hitting snooze every morning for 30 minutes equals 7 full workdays a year.

Time is always compounding. You're either compounding wealth through smart use or compounding poverty through waste.

Corporate POV vs. Street POV

Corporate POV: Employees who waste time at work — gossip, endless breaks, procrastination — stay stuck. The ones who manage time, prioritize tasks, and use downtime to sharpen skills rise faster. At higher levels, executives pay thousands for time coaches, assistants, and systems because they know wasted minutes equal millions lost.

Street POV: Hustlers who waste daylight hours sleeping off last night's party miss the best moves. Deals happen early. Opportunities strike fast. Those who respect time survive. Those who waste it chasing women, drama, or petty distractions die broke. On the block, time is literally life or death — delay one second too long, and you could lose both.

Both worlds reveal the same truth: how you spend time decides how you spend life.

The Psychology of Procrastination

Psychologists explain procrastination as "temporal discounting" — the brain favors short-term pleasure over long-term gain. That's why so many people scroll instead of study, party instead of plan, sleep instead of strategize. The brain tricks you into believing you'll "catch up later." But later doesn't exist. Later becomes never.

A Parable: The Leaky Hourglass

A man inherited a magical hourglass. Every grain of sand was a chance at wealth. But the man wasted the sand on parties and sleep. One day, the last grain fell, and the man begged for more. The hourglass stayed silent. His time was gone, forever.

Case Study: The Student Who Split Paths

Two students graduated together. One spent his twenties working, networking, and investing. The other spent his twenties partying, traveling aimlessly, and living "for the moment." At thirty-five, the first had built assets and stability. The second had memories but no money, wisdom but no wealth. Both had the same time. One invested it. One wasted it.

Predictions if Unchecked

If time mismanagement continues, generations will keep wasting their most powerful resource. The young will give away their prime years for entertainment. The middle-aged will waste decades in survival cycles. The old will regret what they didn't build.

In twenty years, the divide will be brutal: those who managed time will live free. Those who wasted it will live bitter. The cruel truth? Poverty in old age often isn't from lack of money — it's from lack of time discipline when it mattered most.

Strategies to Break the Trap

Audit Your Day: Track where every hour goes. Awareness is step one.

Prioritize Peak Hours: Use your best energy times for your most important work.

Schedule Growth: Block time daily for skill-building, planning, or networking.

Kill Time Vampires: Gossip, endless scrolling, aimless outings — cut them out like cancers.

Respect Mortality: Remember: your time isn't infinite. Treat every day like an investment.

Closing Manifesto

Time is the only true currency. Waste it, and no paycheck can save you. Invest it, and even with little money, you'll build wealth.

Every hour you waste feeds someone else's dream. Every hour you invest feeds your own. The clock is not your friend. It is your creditor. And it collects daily.

Respect time. Master time. Or be buried by time.

Chapter 22 – The Death of Curiosity

The moment you stop asking questions, you stop growing. The moment you stop exploring, you stop evolving. And the moment curiosity dies, wealth dies with it.

Curiosity is the spark behind every invention, every business idea, every strategy that changes the world. The people who stay curious become lifelong students, constantly learning, adapting, and multiplying their opportunities. The people who kill their curiosity become fossils while still alive — stuck in old ways, outdated skills, and expired opportunities.

The death of curiosity is one of the most silent wealth killers, because it feels comfortable. People convince themselves they already know enough. They say, "I'm too old to learn," or "That's just how it is." And with those words, they bury their potential.

Comfort as a Coffin

Comfort kills more dreams than failure. Curiosity demands discomfort. It requires admitting ignorance, asking questions, risking embarrassment. Most people avoid that. They'd rather stick with what's familiar, even if it keeps them broke, than explore something new that could make them free.

Every wealthy innovator, hustler, or leader was curious first. They asked:

What if there's a better way?

What if I try this?

What if I learn that skill?
The broke majority never asks.

Corporate POV vs. Street POV

Corporate POV: Employees who stop learning stagnate. They master one system, one role, and cling to it for decades. Meanwhile, industries change, companies collapse, and they're left jobless. The curious employees — the ones who read, take courses, ask questions, and explore — become irreplaceable. Their curiosity compounds into promotions, leadership roles, and influence.

Street POV: On the block, hustlers who stop learning die. The ones who never study new laws, new hustles, new markets, or new technologies get caught slipping. Meanwhile, the curious hustlers who ask questions, who adapt, who learn beyond the streets, escape the block altogether. Curiosity separates survivors from statistics.

Both sides prove the same rule: curiosity is wealth. Its death is poverty.

The Psychology of Curiosity

Neuroscience shows curiosity lights up the brain's reward system. It makes learning addictive. But when curiosity is killed — by shame, fear, or routine — the brain becomes stagnant. People stop seeking growth, and the mind decays. The wealthy fuel curiosity like firewood. The broke let it burn out.

A Parable: The Locked Library

A village had a great library filled with books of wisdom. The doors were open, but most villagers walked past daily, never stepping inside. Only a few entered, reading, questioning, learning. Years later, those few became leaders, inventors, and builders. The rest stayed peasants, blind to the treasure beside them. The library wasn't locked. Their minds were.

Case Study: The Factory Worker vs. the Tinkerer

Derrick worked in a factory for 25 years. He learned the job once and never asked for more. When machines replaced his role, he was left behind.

Meanwhile, Javier started in the same factory but stayed curious. He learned how the machines worked, asked supervisors about management, and studied business in his off time. When automation hit, Javier transitioned into training and later started his own repair company. Same starting point, different ending. The difference was curiosity.

Predictions if Unchecked

If curiosity keeps dying, communities will remain trapped in ignorance, unable to compete in a fast-changing world. Industries will move on, leaving whole populations obsolete. People will become slaves to technology they never bothered to understand.

In twenty years, the wealth gap will be defined not by money, but by mindset. Those who stay curious will surf every wave of change. Those who kill curiosity will drown beneath it.

Strategies to Break the Trap

Ask More Questions: Never settle for "that's how it is." Dig deeper.

Learn Daily: Books, courses, podcasts, mentors — curiosity thrives on fuel.

Explore Beyond Comfort: Try new places, people, and skills. Growth hides in discomfort.

Challenge Beliefs: Curiosity requires questioning your own assumptions.

Model Children: Kids ask "why" endlessly. Adults should, too.

Financial illiteracy is not an accident. It is an industry. It is a quiet machine built into the foundation of society, designed to make sure the majority of people never learn how money works — while a small minority profits off their ignorance. You can call it a system, but I call it a weapon. Because what else do you call something that drains entire communities, erases generational wealth, and convinces people that being broke is just their fault?

Let's be real: schools teach you how to memorize facts, obey bells, and prepare for tests. They don't teach you how to negotiate a salary, how compound interest grows, or how to protect your family's land. Most people graduate knowing the Pythagorean theorem but unable to explain a mortgage. That is not by accident. That is design.

Economists Lusardi and Mitchell call financial literacy a form of "human capital." And guess what? The less you have, the less wealth you accumulate over your lifetime. In plain terms: if you don't know how money works, your ignorance is worth billions to someone else. Your lack of knowledge is their steady paycheck.

Why They Don't Teach It

Why don't schools teach money? Ask yourself: who profits from an educated consumer? Who profits when you can read contracts, build credit, invest in yourself, and refuse predatory loans? Not the banks. Not the payday lenders. Not the student loan companies. Not the credit card giants. They profit when you don't know.

A teacher can lose their job for discussing "politics" in school, but a high school can partner with Coca-Cola and plaster vending machines in the hallway.

Kids leave school without learning how to file taxes but can recite all the amendments on the Bill of Rights.

History classes teach you about wars but not about how those wars were funded by debt markets and bonds.

The truth is, keeping you financially ignorant keeps the machine running. Because an ignorant worker accepts whatever wage is offered. An ignorant borrower signs whatever loan is available. An ignorant consumer spends without budgeting. Ignorance is the fuel of capitalism.

The Cost of Ignorance

Let's put numbers on it.

A 25-year-old who invests $200 a month at 8% returns will have over $700,000 by retirement. The same 25-year-old who never learns to invest? Maybe $20,000 in a savings account. The difference is almost a million dollars — not from talent, but from knowledge.

The average payday loan of $375 ends up costing $520 in fees. That's a 391% APR. And millions of Americans sign these contracts every year, not because they're dumb, but because nobody ever showed them alternatives.

Black farmers in the 1900s lost over 14 million acres of land not because they lacked talent in farming, but because they lacked access to legal literacy and documentation. No deeds, no records, no defense.

Ignorance has a dollar value. And it is one of the most profitable industries on Earth.

Corporate POV vs. Street POV
Corporate Perspective

Corporations love financial ignorance. It keeps employees passive and customers dependent. Let's break it down:

Retirement Plans: Corporations know most employees won't contribute or maximize their 401(k). That means less matching money they have to give away.

Credit Cards: Credit companies thrive because customers don't calculate compounding interest. They just see a minimum payment and assume it's manageable.

Contracts: Companies bury terms in legal jargon. They know 90% of people will never read or fully understand the fine print.

In the boardroom, ignorance is an asset. The less you know, the more they profit.

Street Perspective

On the streets, financial ignorance looks different but cuts just as deep.

The Hustler: A man flips sneakers without tracking inventory or taxes. He makes cash but never builds credit or a paper trail. Five years later, he has nothing to show lenders, nothing to scale, nothing to leverage.

The Artist: A young rapper signs away publishing rights for $25,000. The label profits millions off his work, while he stays broke. That's financial illiteracy turned into slavery.

The Single Mother: She works three jobs but never learns how to budget or build credit. She cashes checks at predatory spots, pays 5–10% fees each time, and loses thousands over her lifetime.

The corporate world robs with contracts. The street world robs with quick deals. Both rob you through ignorance.

The Psychology of Illiteracy

Financial illiteracy is not just about lacking information — it's about psychological programming.

Shame: People feel embarrassed about money, so they avoid asking questions.

Taboo: Families don't talk about money at the dinner table. Parents pass on silence, not knowledge.

Fear: Many believe money is too complicated for them. They fear looking stupid, so they stay ignorant.

Culture: Consumer culture pushes people to spend instead of invest, flex instead of plan.

These psychological traps ensure people don't seek education, even when it's available. They protect the system.

Parable: The Two Villages

There were two villages. In the first, the elders taught children how to plant seeds, save grain, and track seasons. In the second, the elders told children not to worry, that food would "work itself out." Years later, the first village thrived, with silos of grain, trade networks, and stability. The second village starved every winter.

When asked why they didn't prepare, the starving villagers said, "Nobody told us how."

Ignorance wasn't their choice. It was their inheritance.

Case Studies: The Cost of Not Knowing

Mortgage Crisis 2008 – Millions signed subprime loans with ballooning interest rates they didn't understand. Banks collapsed the global economy, but homeowners bore the brunt. Ignorance turned into foreclosure.

The Tuskegee Airmen – Skilled Black pilots returning from WWII were denied GI Bill benefits because they couldn't navigate the paperwork. Many white veterans leveraged it to build generational wealth. Documentation literacy divided futures.

Immigrant Families – Many immigrant groups built wealth by pooling resources and teaching each other how to navigate banks, taxes, and ownership. Communities that lacked this literacy lost ground.

Predictions if Unchecked

If financial illiteracy continues unchecked:

AI and algorithms will widen the gap. People who don't understand digital finance will be excluded from opportunities.

Predatory lending will evolve. Instead of payday loans, it'll be microloans through apps with hidden fees.

Generations will inherit ignorance. Families will keep living paycheck to paycheck while wealth consolidates at the top.

Without intervention, ignorance will become a caste system. Those who know will rule. Those who don't will serve.

Strategies for Liberation

Make Money Talk Normal: Break the silence in families. Talk budgets, taxes, and credit at the dinner table.

Demand Curriculum: Push schools to teach money like math. If they don't, teach it in communities, churches, and online.

Community Literacy Hubs: Create spaces where people can share resources on taxes, grants, contracts, and credit repair.

Leverage Technology: Budgeting apps, credit monitoring, robo-advisors — use the tools, but also learn how they work.

Document Everything: Keep receipts, contracts, and records. Paperwork is memory, and memory is power.

Mentorship: Seek out those who've mastered money and learn. Not influencers flexing cars, but people building quietly.

Closing Manifesto

Curiosity is the lifeblood of growth. Kill it, and you kill progress. Starve it, and you starve wealth. The death of curiosity is the death of opportunity itself.

Stay hungry. Stay questioning. Stay uncomfortable. Because the world doesn't reward those who know it all — it rewards those who never stop learning.

Wealth belongs to the curious. Poverty belongs to the content.

Chapter 23 – The Poverty of Imagination

Before you ever hold wealth in your hand, you must hold it in your head. But most people's imaginations are bankrupt long before their wallets are. They can't dream past survival. They can't see beyond rent, bills, and weekend fun. They lack vision, so they lack direction. And without direction, wealth never comes.

The poverty of imagination is not just an individual issue — it's systemic. Schools train obedience, not creativity. Media feeds you struggle stories, not possibility. Whole communities are programmed to believe their ceiling is low, and over time, they stop even trying to look up.

Wealth requires imagination. Every empire, every invention, every breakthrough started as a dream. The poor stop dreaming, and that's why they stay poor.

The Cost of a Small Mind

A man who only dreams of buying sneakers will never own the store. A woman who only dreams of paying rent will never own real estate. A hustler who only dreams of surviving the week will never build a legacy.

Small dreams create small moves. And small moves guarantee small lives. The poverty of imagination doesn't just shrink goals — it shrinks identity. You become what you believe, and if you believe small, you live small.

Corporate POV vs. Street POV

Corporate POV: The worker who only imagines a promotion will always be capped. The worker who imagines owning the company, starting their own, or building something bigger will eventually outgrow the system. Companies love small imaginations because it keeps employees from ever leaving.

Street POV: On the block, the hustler who only imagines fast money dies broke or in prison. The one who imagines flipping illegal hustle into legal empire creates generational wealth. The block kills dreamers who can't see past chains. The streets reward those who can imagine freedom.

Both sides prove the same law: imagination is blueprint. Without it, you're just a worker for someone else's dream.

The Psychology of Limited Vision

Psychologists call it "learned helplessness." When people face constant setbacks, they eventually stop trying new things, convinced nothing will change. Over time, this shrinks imagination. Kids grow up with big dreams — astronaut, doctor, entrepreneur. Adults shrink down to "I just hope I get by." That shrinkage is the poverty of imagination at work.

It's not that they can't dream. It's that they've been convinced it's pointless.

A Parable: The Two Windows

Two prisoners sat in cells. One window faced a wall, and the man spent his days staring at bricks. The other window faced the sky, and the man spent his days staring at clouds. One dreamed of escape, one didn't. When the door was left unlocked one night, the man staring at the wall stayed. The man staring at the sky left. Imagination freed him before the door did.

Case Study: Oprah vs. The Average Worker

Oprah Winfrey grew up in poverty, abuse, and trauma. Most in her situation could only imagine survival. But Oprah imagined stages, microphones, global audiences. Her vision guided her to build an empire.

Meanwhile, millions of equally talented people never left their neighborhoods because they never imagined it was possible. Same potential. Different imagination.

Predictions if Unchecked

If the poverty of imagination continues, whole generations will stay locked in cycles of small thinking. Communities will keep passing down survival mindsets while other groups pass down ownership. Opportunities will exist, but they'll never be seen because people won't believe they're possible.

In twenty years, the wealth gap won't just be money. It'll be imagination. Those who dreamed will live free. Those who didn't will still be renting, working, and surviving.

Strategies to Break the Trap

Expand Exposure: Travel, read, explore. New sights expand imagination.

Dream Beyond Bills: Goals should extend past survival into legacy.

Visualize Daily: Spend time picturing wealth, freedom, and success in detail. Train your mind to see bigger.

Study Dreamers: Read biographies of builders, innovators, and leaders. Borrow their imagination.

Protect Vision: Share dreams only with those who feed them. Doubters shrink imagination.

Documentation doesn't sound glamorous. It's not sexy like "investing," it doesn't feel urgent like "debt." But make no mistake — failure to document is one of the most brutal, overlooked killers of wealth. Paperwork is power. Receipts are shields. Contracts are weapons. Without them, your history can be erased, your rights ignored, your property stolen.

Wealth is built on paper. Deeds, titles, contracts, invoices, journals, and ledgers are the skeleton of capitalism. And yet millions of people, especially in marginalized communities, live undocumented lives when it comes to money. They hustle, they grind, they save cash under the mattress, but without records it's like building a mansion on sand. One flood, one fire, one legal battle — and it all disappears.

Why Documentation Matters

The system doesn't respect your word. It respects your paperwork.

Your handshake doesn't hold in court. Contracts do.

Your memory doesn't earn you a tax refund. Receipts do.

Your bloodline doesn't protect your land. Deeds do.

Documentation is proof. Without it, you are invisible to the system. And invisibility means vulnerability.

Corporate POV vs. Street POV
Corporate Perspective

Corporations don't play casual with documentation. They document EVERYTHING. Meetings, transactions, decisions, patents, copyrights, and even casual ideas are timestamped and filed. Why? Because paper trails equal power.

Contracts: Corporations never hire without them. They know contracts protect their interests.

Receipts: Every expense is logged, categorized, and leveraged for tax write-offs.

Intellectual Property: Corporations patent ideas before they even exist, locking down profit potential before competition arises.

In corporate America, the motto is: "If it's not written down, it doesn't exist."

Street Perspective

On the block, it's the opposite. Deals are verbal. Handshakes are common. Trust is assumed. Documentation is seen as "square," "snitching," or just unnecessary.

A hustler sells product but never tracks inventory. He doesn't realize how much he's losing until he's broke.

A barber cuts hair for 10 years in cash but has no records. When he tries to buy a home, the bank says, "We can't verify your income."

A Black family owns farmland for generations but never formalized deeds. Developers come in, challenge ownership, and the family loses acres because they can't prove documentation.

One world thrives on documentation. The other starves without it.

Historical Erasure Through Lack of Paperwork

Black Land Loss in America

Between 1910 and today, Black farmers lost over 14 million acres of land. Why? Because they lacked wills, deeds, and legal representation. Land was passed down "informally," and when heirs couldn't prove ownership, white developers, banks, or even the government seized it. That wasn't incompetence — it was a failure to document weaponized against them.

Native Land Theft

Tribes signed treaties under duress, often without full documentation or under fraudulent terms. The U.S. government exploited the lack of paperwork literacy to steal millions of acres.

Immigrant Advantage

In contrast, many immigrant groups built wealth by obsessively documenting. Ledgers, cooperative savings logs, and business receipts became proof of creditworthiness. Banks extended loans because they could verify records. Communities that documented thrived. Those that didn't, lost everything.

The Psychology of "No Paperwork"

Why do so many avoid documentation?

Trust Culture: Some communities rely on verbal agreements because "a man's word is bond." But the system doesn't honor that.

Shame: People who operate informally fear documentation will expose their lack of compliance or legality.

Ignorance: Many simply don't know what's required until it's too late.

Rebellion: Some see documentation as "feeding the system." But rejecting paperwork doesn't destroy the system — it only destroys your claim within it.

The sad reality is this: failure to document is not rebellion, it's self-erasure.

Parable: The Carpenter's Work

A carpenter built houses for 30 years. Each client paid cash. He trusted his reputation would stand as proof of his work. One day, a wealthy man accused him of botching a project from 10 years ago. The carpenter swore he never built that house. The court asked for contracts, receipts, or blueprints. He had none. The wealthy man showed paperwork. The carpenter lost everything.

The carpenter's skill was never in question. His lack of documentation erased his truth.

Case Studies

Prince and His Masters

Prince famously fought to own his music masters because record labels had contracts. They documented ownership. Prince had performance, creativity, and culture — but without the right paperwork, he didn't own the very songs he created.

The Informal Business Owner

A woman runs a catering business for years in cash. She feeds weddings, churches, and entire neighborhoods. But when COVID hits and government aid becomes available, she can't apply. No tax returns, no records. Her business starves while "official" ones thrive.

The Lottery Winner

Multiple stories exist of lottery winners losing fortunes because they failed to document who was entitled to shares, how money was managed, or what agreements were made. Millions gone to lawsuits.

Predictions if Unchecked

If failure to document continues:

Land Loss Will Continue: Families will keep losing homes and property without wills and deeds.

Business Exclusion: Entrepreneurs will continue to be locked out of loans, grants, and partnerships.

Cultural Theft: Creators will keep losing rights to music, art, and inventions. Corporations will profit off communities that don't protect intellectual property.

The future is clear: those who document will dominate. Those who don't will disappear.

Strategies to Protect Yourself

Write Wills: Even a simple written will can protect your children and heirs.

Keep Receipts: Track every transaction. Paper or digital, but keep it.

Register Businesses: Even side hustles deserve legal structure. An LLC protects you.

Record Deals: Never rely on verbal promises. Get it in writing.

Protect IP: If you create, file copyrights, trademarks, or patents. Don't assume culture protects you.

Journal Your Progress: Keep a record of moves. One day it can defend your legacy.

Closing Manifesto

The richest people aren't the smartest. They're the biggest dreamers. The poorest people aren't the laziest. They're the smallest dreamers.

Imagination is wealth's blueprint. Without it, you're building nothing.

So dare to dream beyond survival. Dare to imagine yourself free. Dare to think bigger than your neighborhood, your job, your bank account. Because if you can't see wealth in your mind, you'll never hold it in your hand.

The poverty of imagination is worse than financial poverty. Heal it, and you heal everything.

Chapter 24 – Failure to Document

Paperwork is memory. Documentation is leverage. Yet most people treat record-keeping like an afterthought, a chore they'll "get to later." That laziness costs more wealth than theft ever could. Because without documentation, you can't prove ownership, you can't enforce rights, and you can't pass legacy.

Failure to document is why families lose property, why businesses collapse, and why opportunities vanish. Oral stories fade. Handshakes disappear. Promises break. But paper — signed, sealed, and stored — lasts. Wealth lives on paper. Poverty thrives in memory.

The Price of Forgetting

When you don't keep receipts, you can't fight fraud.

When you don't keep contracts, you can't enforce deals.

When you don't keep journals, you can't measure growth.

When you don't keep wills, your family fights over scraps after you die.

Documentation is boring until it saves your life. But by then, most people don't have it.

Corporate POV vs. Street POV

Corporate POV: Corporations document everything. Meetings have minutes. Deals have contracts. Even bathroom breaks get logged. Why? Because documentation is protection and leverage. Employees, however, rarely document. They don't save offer letters, track hours, or keep proof of promises. When disputes come, corporations have paperwork, and workers have memory. Guess who wins?

Street POV: Hustlers without paperwork lose faster than they hustle. No receipts means no proof. No contracts means no enforcement. Rappers without copyrights lose royalties. Land without deeds gets stolen. Hustlers who play the game without paper are hustling on sand. Meanwhile, the sharp ones trademark, patent, LLC, and file everything. They don't just hustle — they own.

Both worlds prove the same law: paperwork is profit. The absence of paperwork is poverty.

The Psychology of Avoidance

Psychologists call it "present bias." People avoid tasks that feel tedious now, even if they save pain later. Documentation feels tedious. But that short-term avoidance creates long-term chaos. Avoiding paperwork is really avoiding responsibility. And avoiding responsibility is avoiding wealth.

A Parable: The Two Brothers' Land

Two brothers inherited land from their father. One documented the deed, filed it, and protected it. The other trusted memory and community respect. Years later, developers came. The documented brother kept his land and leveraged it into millions. The undocumented brother lost everything to outsiders with paperwork. The land was the same. The difference was the paper.

Case Study: Black Farmers vs. the System

For decades, Black farmers in America lost millions of acres. Not because they lacked skill. Not because they didn't work hard. But because they lacked documentation. Without clear deeds, wills, or records, land was stolen legally. Families argued, courts intervened, and corporations swooped in. Failure to document destroyed generational wealth.

On the flip side, immigrants arriving with little often documented everything — receipts, taxes, business filings. That documentation opened doors to loans, ownership, and legal protection. They built wealth not just with work, but with paper.

Predictions if Unchecked

If people keep failing to document, they'll keep losing in silence. Families will lose inheritances. Communities will lose land. Businesses will collapse without records. Courts will side with whoever has paper, not whoever has truth.

In twenty years, wealth gaps will widen not just by money, but by memory. The documented will build legacy. The undocumented will disappear from history.

Strategies to Break the Trap

Save Receipts & Records: From small purchases to major deals, keep proof.

Write Everything Down: Meetings, promises, goals, and progress. Memory fades. Paper doesn't.

Use Contracts Always: Don't trust handshakes. Even with family. Especially with family.

Create Wills & Trusts: Protect your assets for your heirs. Don't let courts decide.

Organize Documentation: Digital and physical folders. Easy access is power.

Every click, every search, every scroll, every "like" is building your digital identity. Not the one you think you have — the one the system assigns you. Algorithms are not neutral. They are designed to categorize, predict, and control. Whether you know it or not, your digital shadow is already being used to decide what ads you see, what jobs you qualify for, what loans you're approved for, and even what opportunities you'll never hear about.

Your online footprint is not just data — it's a financial profile. And the brutal truth is this: if you don't understand how digital identity and algorithms shape your future, you're already being silently robbed of opportunities.

What Is Digital Identity?

Digital identity is the sum of your online behavior:

Social media posts

Browsing history

Shopping habits

Location data

Contacts and networks

Even how long you pause on a picture

Corporations and governments track it, package it, and sell it. Then algorithms decide what you're worth. To them, you're not human. You're a dataset.

The Algorithmic Trap

Algorithms control your environment in ways you don't even see:

Job Applications: AI hiring systems scan résumés for keywords. If you don't match the algorithm's filters, your application is deleted before a human even sees it.

Credit Scoring: Alternative data is being used to judge you — including your shopping patterns, subscriptions, and even your social media networks.

Advertising: Algorithms push payday loan ads to broke communities and investment ads to wealthier ones. Your environment is shaped to reinforce your status.

Policing: Predictive policing software targets neighborhoods based on historical data — usually where poor and Black people live — ensuring cycles of over-policing never end.

This is not coincidence. This is digital redlining.

Corporate POV vs. Street POV

Corporate Perspective

Corporations live off data. Data is the new oil, the new gold. Tech giants don't sell products; they sell you.

Facebook/Meta: Makes billions selling your behavioral profile to advertisers.

Banks: Use AI to decide who gets loans, who doesn't, and at what rate. Bias in the algorithm means bias in real life.

Employers: Save time and money by letting AI filter résumés — but this automation kills candidates who don't fit digital molds.

Corporations use algorithms not to serve you, but to serve their bottom line.

Street Perspective

On the streets, algorithms show up in brutal ways:

Young hustlers trying to promote music get shadowbanned because their content triggers filters.

Job seekers in the hood never even get call-backs because AI hiring tools throw out résumés from zip codes tied to "low productivity."

Police flood Black neighborhoods because predictive software says crime "might" happen there, even when the algorithm is just recycling old arrest data.

On the street, algorithmic control looks like invisible bars. You can't see them, but you feel them.

The Psychology of Digital Control

Algorithms are designed to prey on psychology.

Addiction: Platforms track dopamine responses. They know what makes you scroll longer, so they feed you more of it.

Confirmation Bias: Algorithms feed you what you already believe, keeping you stuck in intellectual bubbles.

Comparison Traps: Social media pushes flex culture, making you spend more to keep up with images of wealth that aren't even real.

Fear: Algorithms decide which headlines you see, often prioritizing fear and outrage because it keeps you online.

The result? People feel like they have "free will" online while being programmed like lab rats.

Parable: The Invisible Shepherd

A flock of sheep grazed in an open field. They thought they were free because no fences surrounded them. But above, a shepherd on a hill used whistles the sheep couldn't hear. Every time they strayed too far, he whistled, and the sheep turned back without realizing why. They believed their choices were their own.

The shepherd never built a fence. He didn't need to.

Case Studies

Amazon Hiring Algorithm

Amazon built an AI to filter résumés. It learned from historical data — which favored men. The result? It downgraded women's résumés automatically. Talent was erased by bias.

Credit Algorithms in China

China's "social credit system" ties financial access to digital behavior. Late payments, political criticism, or even associating with "risky" friends lowers your score. Imagine losing a loan because of who you text.

Target's Pregnancy Prediction

Target once predicted a teenage girl was pregnant based on her shopping habits. They mailed her coupons for baby products before her own family knew. Algorithms know you better than you know yourself.

YouTube Radicalization

People searching for harmless topics end up funneled into extremist or hyper-consumerist rabbit holes because algorithms prioritize engagement over truth. This shapes not only identity but spending patterns.

Predictions if Unchecked

If algorithmic control continues unchecked:

Permanent Digital Redlining: Whole zip codes and races will be locked into low-credit, low-opportunity digital cages.

Automated Poverty: Jobs, loans, and opportunities will increasingly be filtered by biased AI, keeping marginalized people permanently excluded.

Loss of Autonomy: Algorithms will decide what you buy, who you date, and how you vote. Free will will become an illusion.

Digital Slavery: Data will be the chain. You won't need shackles when every decision you make is predicted and profited from.

Strategies for Liberation

Control Your Data: Limit what you share. Use privacy tools, VPNs, and encrypted apps.

Understand Algorithms: Study how platforms work. Don't assume what you see online is neutral.

Diversify Information: Break out of algorithmic bubbles. Read, watch, and listen outside what is fed to you.

Own Your Digital Identity: Build a professional footprint — résumés, portfolios, and websites you control, not just social media.

Document Offline: Keep paper trails in addition to digital ones. Algorithms can erase; paper proves.

Community Defense: Advocate for algorithm transparency laws. Push for audits that expose bias in digital systems.

Monetize Intentionally: Don't just give data away. Learn how to leverage your footprint for business, marketing, or branding.

Closing Manifesto

The difference between wealth and poverty is often a single sheet of paper. One signature can build empires. One missing document can erase them.

Stop treating documentation like a chore. Treat it like currency. Because when the fight comes — and it always comes — the paper wins.

Document your hustle. Document your growth. Document your legacy. Or watch your name, your work, and your wealth vanish into silence.

Chapter 25 – Not Speaking Up to the Necessary People for Help

Closed mouths don't get fed — but running your mouth to the wrong people leaves you starving. Too many people cry for help in the wrong direction. They vent to friends with no power, complain to co-workers with no influence, or rant on social media where no solution lives. They rarely speak to the actual people or institutions that can change their situation.

This isn't just about pride. It's about laziness, ignorance, and misplaced comfort. It feels good to talk about your problems to someone who will sympathize — but sympathy doesn't solve. Strategy does. And failing to ask the right people for help is a silent wealth killer.

The Hidden Cost of Misplaced Conversations

Talking to broke friends about money doesn't build wealth.

Complaining to co-workers about your boss won't change your pay.

Ranting online about injustice doesn't fix contracts, credit, or careers.

All it does is waste time, spread negativity, and sometimes even ruin reputation. Meanwhile, the people who could've helped — mentors, lenders, lawyers, leaders — never even heard your voice.

Corporate POV vs. Street POV

Corporate POV: Employees vent in the break room but never walk into HR with documented complaints. They gossip about unfair pay but never negotiate with managers. They ask peers for financial advice but never talk to accountants. The result? Years of frustration, no change.

Street POV: On the block, hustlers complain about lack of opportunity to the same broke friends they grew up with. They beg favors from people who have no resources, instead of finding mentors, investors, or legal advice. The ones who level up aren't louder — they're smarter. They speak to the plug, not the peanut gallery.

Both sides prove the same truth: talking without strategy is therapy without healing.

The Psychology of Laziness

Psychologists call it "social surrogacy." People talk to others about problems as a way of feeling relief, even if nothing changes. It's easier to vent than to research. It's easier to gossip than to make a phone call to the person in power. Comfort kills progress, and fear of rejection keeps mouths shut where they matter most.

A Parable: The Beggar at the Well

A beggar cried daily about thirst. He told everyone in the village of his suffering. Neighbors nodded, sympathized, and went about their day. One day, a traveler asked, "Why don't you speak to the man who owns the well?" The beggar replied, "I didn't think he'd listen." The traveler went to the well owner, asked, and water was given. The beggar died of thirst with a crowd of listeners, but no solution.

Case Study: The Job Seeker

Maya applied to jobs online for years with no luck. She vented to friends, cried to family, and posted frustration on Facebook. Nothing changed. One day, she finally reached out to a former professor for a recommendation. That single message landed her an interview she'd been chasing for five years. The difference wasn't luck. It was asking the right person.

Meanwhile, Darnell, a hustler, complained daily about police harassment. He told everyone but never went to legal aid clinics or organizations that fought cases for free. He spent years bitter, but never strategic. His silence to the right people killed opportunities he never knew existed.

Predictions if Unchecked

If people keep talking sideways instead of upward, communities will stay locked in cycles of complaint. Gossip will multiply while solutions die in silence. The powerful will remain untouched, never challenged or asked. And the voiceless will stay broke, frustrated, and ignored.

In twenty years, the wealth gap will widen not just because of resources, but because of communication. The bold who speak to power will rise. The silent or misdirected will drown in echo chambers of complaint.

Strategies to Break the Trap

Identify Gatekeepers: Know who actually has the power to solve your problem. Focus there.

Speak with Evidence: Document before you speak. Bring receipts, facts, and clarity.

Ask Directly: Don't hint, don't whine. Make clear requests to the right people.

Stop Venting to the Powerless: If they can't change your situation, limit the energy you give them.

Build Resource Maps: Keep a list of contacts, mentors, institutions, and services that can provide solutions.

Geography is one of the most underestimated wealth killers in existence. Where you live decides more about your financial future than almost anything else. Not your talent. Not your grind. Not your dreams. Geography determines the jobs available, the people you meet, the schools your kids attend, the health care you get, the safety of your block, the air you breathe, and the wealth you can build.

This is the trap: you think you chose where you live, but most of the time geography chose you. Zip codes act like cages, locking generations into cycles of poverty or privilege. And the sickest part? The system was designed this way.

Redlining: The Original Map of Poverty

In the 1930s, federal agencies created maps grading neighborhoods for investment. "Good" neighborhoods got loans, schools, and infrastructure. "Bad" neighborhoods — often Black and immigrant communities — were outlined in red. Banks denied loans there, investors avoided them, and property values plummeted.

That wasn't 100 years ago history. That was policy. And the aftershock is still alive today:

Homes in formerly redlined areas are worth less than half of those in "greenlined" areas, even now.

Black families lost billions in generational wealth because their homes never appreciated.

White families in "good" zones leveraged equity to send kids to college, start businesses, and pass wealth forward.

Geography wasn't just fate. It was engineered.

Corporate POV vs. Street POV
Corporate Perspective

For corporations, geography is opportunity. They place stores, billboards, and factories strategically:

Fast Food: Saturated in poor neighborhoods, fueling obesity and long-term health costs.

Banks vs. Check-Cashers: Wealthier areas get banks and credit unions; poor neighborhoods get payday lenders.

Retail: High-income areas get Whole Foods and Apple Stores; poor areas get dollar stores and liquor stores.

Corporations know geography dictates consumption. They exploit it with precision.

Street Perspective

On the street, geography is survival. The block you live on can determine whether you get pulled over, whether your hustle thrives, or whether you make it to 30.

A hustler on the wrong block is trapped — high police presence, no foot traffic, no mentors.

Kids in poor zip codes are more likely to attend underfunded schools, more likely to drop out, and less likely to land high-paying jobs.

Even bus routes and train lines decide who gets to commute to opportunity and who stays stuck.

On the street, geography is destiny.

The Psychology of Location

Geography also shapes mindset.

Exposure: If all you see is poverty, you assume wealth is impossible.

Normalization: If everyone around you struggles, you think struggle is natural.

Aspiration: If you grow up in neighborhoods with doctors, lawyers, and entrepreneurs, you're more likely to become one.

Psychologists call it the "neighborhood effect." People adopt the habits, values, and expectations of those around them. That's why two kids with the same talent can have completely different outcomes — one grows up near Silicon Valley, the other in a rural town with no internet. Geography molds possibility.

Parable: The Two Seeds

A farmer planted two seeds. One fell on rich soil by a river. It grew tall, nourished, and strong. The other fell on dry ground with no water. It struggled, stayed small, and eventually withered.

Both seeds had the same potential. Their geography decided their fate.

Case Studies

Flint, Michigan – Residents were poisoned by their own water system. Geography wasn't just about wealth — it was life and death. Families lost health, jobs, and property value because of where they lived.

Silicon Valley vs. Rural America – A kid in Silicon Valley grows up seeing tech startups, investors, and wealth everywhere. A kid in rural America may never even meet a software engineer. Same IQ, different geography, different outcomes.

Chicago's South Side – Generations of families locked into neighborhoods with underfunded schools, high policing, and food deserts. Meanwhile, wealthier Chicago neighborhoods flourish with resources.

Global South Migration – In the U.S., immigrants from certain countries arrive and cluster in wealth-rich networks. Others, placed in isolated, resource-poor geographies, struggle for generations.

Predictions if Unchecked

If geography traps remain unchecked:

Wealth Gaps Will Explode: Poor areas will stay poor, while rich areas continue building generational wealth.

Climate Change: Poorer neighborhoods will suffer first from flooding, heat, and disasters because infrastructure investment won't reach them.

Digital Divide: Cities with fiber internet and tech hubs will thrive; rural and inner-city communities without them will be left behind.

Mass Incarceration 2.0: Algorithms will target neighborhoods already coded as "high-risk," deepening surveillance and poverty.

Geography will decide destiny more than effort. And the poor will keep hearing "just work harder," while maps dictate their ceiling.

Strategies for Liberation

Mobility: Don't marry your zip code. Seek jobs, schools, and opportunities outside your block.

Collective Investment: Communities can pool resources to buy property and protect against gentrification.

Demand Infrastructure: Fight for better schools, safer water, public transit, and digital access. Geography changes when investment arrives.

Leverage Remote Work: The internet is one of the few tools that can break geographic chains. Learn skills that allow you to earn anywhere.

Create Economic Ecosystems: Build businesses in your area that circulate money inside the community.

Challenge Redlining 2.0: Push back on zoning laws, banking practices, and AI-driven credit discrimination.

Closing Manifesto

Complaints are free. Solutions are costly. And the cost is courage, clarity, and direction. Stop wasting your voice on powerless ears. Speak where it counts. Ask who can answer. Knock on doors that actually open.

Because the brutal truth is this: you're not broke because you never spoke — you're broke because you spoke to the wrong people.

Chapter 26 – Emotional Spending

Money is supposed to be a tool. But for most people, it's therapy. They don't spend to build — they spend to feel. Stress, sadness, boredom, anger, insecurity — every emotion becomes an excuse to swipe. Emotional spending is one of the most common and most overlooked wealth killers, because it disguises itself as self-care, fun, or "deserving a little something."

What people don't realize is that every time they swipe to heal, they dig the wound deeper. Retail therapy doesn't cure depression. Flexing doesn't cure insecurity. Comfort food doesn't cure loneliness. It just empties your wallet and deepens the cycle.

The Cost of Spending Feelings

Buying to flex for others = Debt for applause.

Buying to heal pain = Temporary relief, permanent regret.

Buying out of boredom = Small leaks that drain big dreams.

Every dollar you spend emotionally is a dollar that can't work for you tomorrow. Over time, the habit compounds into credit card debt, missed investments, and wasted years.

Corporate POV vs. Street POV

Corporate POV: Companies weaponize emotions. Ads don't sell products; they sell feelings. That perfume ad isn't about scent — it's about desire. That luxury car commercial isn't about horsepower — it's about status. Corporations know you'll buy based on emotion, then rationalize after. Employees addicted to emotional spending stay trapped in paychecks because they never build savings or investments.

Street POV: Hustlers who spend emotionally die broke. They flip a bag, then blow it on clothes, bottles, and cars to flex for the block. Validation costs everything. Meanwhile, disciplined hustlers reinvest profits, buying tools, property, or businesses. One dies for clout, the other builds for legacy.

Both sides prove the same truth: emotional spending feeds feelings while starving the future.

The Psychology of Emotional Spending

Psychologists call it "affect regulation." When people feel negative emotions, they spend to regulate mood. Buying triggers dopamine, a chemical rush that mimics happiness. But like a drug, the high fades, leaving guilt and emptier pockets. Then the cycle repeats.

It's not just weakness — it's wiring. And unless you break the cycle consciously, you'll stay stuck.

A Parable: The Leaking Roof

A man's roof had a hole. Rain leaked in every storm. Instead of fixing it, he bought new rugs every month to cover the wet floor. He felt good for a while, until the rugs rotted and the house collapsed. His spending hid the pain but never fixed the problem.

That's emotional spending: buying rugs instead of fixing roofs.

Case Study: Lottery Winners and Retail Therapy

Most lottery winners go broke within five years. Why? Emotional spending. They don't invest. They don't strategize. They buy houses for everyone, throw parties, flex cars, and chase feelings. The money disappears faster than it came.

Meanwhile, consider Sarah, a woman who grew up broke. Every time she felt low, she bought clothes she didn't need. When she learned about emotional spending, she shifted. Instead of shopping, she started journaling and exercising. She saved thousands, started a business, and used her money to heal her future instead of her feelings.

Predictions if Unchecked

If emotional spending continues, communities will stay broke, constantly funding corporations but never themselves. Families will pass down debt instead of wealth. Entire generations will stay enslaved to lenders and credit cards, all because they couldn't stop buying for feelings.

In twenty years, the divide will be brutal: some will own assets that pay them, while others will own closets full of clothes that nobody wants.

Strategies to Break the Trap

Pause Before Purchase: Ask: "Am I buying this for utility or emotion?"

Redirect Emotions: Replace shopping with exercise, journaling, prayer, or productive outlets.

Budget Therapy: Set aside small "fun money" so emotions don't wreck the whole budget.

Track Patterns: Notice when emotions trigger spending. Awareness breaks cycles.

Invest Instead of Indulge: Every time you feel the urge to spend emotionally, put that same amount toward savings or tools.

Entertainment is not the enemy. It can inspire, educate, even heal. But addiction to entertainment? That's a silent killer of wealth. It is the thief of hours, the murderer of dreams, the drug that keeps you pacified while your future bleeds out.

Look around. Whole generations have been programmed to consume nonstop: music, video games, sports, streaming, social media, gossip, porn, reality TV. The average person spends more hours a day consuming entertainment than building their legacy. And here's the brutal truth: every hour you give away to meaningless distraction is an hour you can never buy back. Entertainment addiction is engineered slavery with better graphics.

The System Behind the Screen

Entertainment isn't just fun — it's business. Corporations pour billions into studying human psychology to keep you locked in.

Streaming platforms auto-play the next episode, knowing you'll stay seated.

Video games are built with dopamine loops, rewarding you just enough to keep playing.

Social media feeds you endless scrolls of content, keeping you chasing that next hit of novelty.

Sports franchises sell identity and loyalty so deeply that fans spend money and time like soldiers serving a flag.

The system doesn't want you to just watch. It wants you addicted. Because an addicted viewer doesn't build. An addicted viewer buys.

Corporate POV vs. Street POV

Corporate Perspective

Entertainment corporations are the biggest dealers in the world. They manufacture dopamine like factories manufacture steel. Their business model is distraction-as-profit.

Netflix, YouTube, TikTok, Twitch — all competing for your attention because your attention is money.

The NFL, NBA, and global sports leagues sell not just games but lifestyles, merchandise, and loyalty.

Record labels profit more from viral dances and catchy hooks than from meaningful art.

Corporations don't care if you stay broke, tired, or lost — as long as you keep watching.

Street Perspective

On the street, entertainment addiction kills in different ways.

Young men spend hours gaming, flexing online, or watching sports instead of learning trades or starting hustles.

Communities obsess over celebrity gossip while ignoring local politics that shape their actual lives.

Social media becomes a stage where people act rich instead of getting rich, chasing likes while losing decades.

On the street, entertainment isn't just a distraction. It's anesthesia. It numbs the pain of poverty while deepening it.

The Psychology of Distraction

Entertainment addiction works because it hijacks your brain's reward system.

Dopamine Loops: Small, repeatable hits of pleasure trick your brain into thinking progress is happening.

Escape Mechanism: People stuck in survival use entertainment to escape pain. But escape without strategy is just avoidance.

Identity Projection: Fans merge their self-worth with teams, celebrities, or influencers. When their team wins, they feel accomplished — even though nothing in their life changed.

Peer Pressure: Culture normalizes wasting time on entertainment. If you don't binge the latest show, you're "out of the loop."

It's not weakness. It's science. Addiction is built into the system.

Parable: The Feast of Distractions

A king feared rebellion from the poor. His advisors suggested new laws, new armies, new taxes. But the king instead built a giant theater and offered free plays every night. The people came, laughed, cried, and cheered. They were so entertained they forgot their hunger, their oppression, their chains. The king ruled unchallenged, not with swords, but with stories.

Case Studies

Roman Empire – Bread and Circuses

Rome kept the masses calm by offering food and nonstop entertainment in coliseums. While people cheered gladiators, corruption and collapse spread behind the scenes. Sound familiar?

The Sports Economy

Billions of dollars circulate around sports. Players become multimillionaires, but fans spend hundreds on tickets, jerseys, and subscriptions. Families in debt still prioritize cable just to watch games. Loyalty to entertainment outweighs loyalty to wealth.

Video Game Addiction in Asia

In countries like China and South Korea, gaming addiction is so severe that governments imposed curfews for youth players. Families reported teens playing 12+ hours a day, destroying health and education.

Social Media Influence

Influencers profit by selling lifestyles. Viewers burn time watching, comparing, and consuming, but rarely create for themselves. Whole careers are built on monetizing the attention of the addicted.

Predictions if Unchecked

If entertainment addiction continues unchecked:

Lost Generations: Entire populations will waste decades binge-watching and scrolling, aging into regret with no assets to show.

Corporate Control: A few mega-corporations will monopolize global culture, dictating not just what people watch but how they think.

Mental Health Crisis: Depression, anxiety, and loneliness will skyrocket as people trade real connection for digital illusion.

Cultural Collapse: Communities will lose identity, relying on media representation instead of self-creation.

Entertainment is not harmless. It is engineered control.

Strategies for Liberation

Set Boundaries: Entertainment in moderation. Schedule it, don't drown in it.

Replace Consumption with Creation: Don't just watch. Create music, stories, videos, or businesses. Turn distraction into profit.

Track Your Hours: Be honest. How many hours a day do you give away? Reclaim them.

Detox Periods: Take breaks from social media, streaming, and gaming to reset your brain's dopamine balance.

Community Focus: Encourage group activities that build — investments, businesses, skill learning — not just watching.

Educate on Manipulation: Teach kids how algorithms and entertainment addiction are designed. Awareness is defense.

Shift Identity: Stop tying self-worth to teams, celebrities, or influencers. Build identity around personal growth.

Closing Manifesto

Money is not a bandage. It's a brick. Every dollar should build something, not just cover pain. Emotional spending keeps you stuck in cycles of healing wounds that never close.

Heal differently. Spend intentionally. Build with discipline. Because if you keep buying for feelings, you'll never buy freedom.

The truth is harsh: emotional spending is emotional slavery. And the only cure is discipline.

Chapter 27 – Fear of Leaving the Crowd

Most people don't fail because they lack talent. They fail because they lack courage to walk away from the crowd. Humans crave belonging. The crowd feels safe, even when the crowd is broke, bitter, and blind. Fear of leaving that comfort zone is one of the deadliest silent wealth killers — because wealth is always outside the herd.

The truth is simple: you can't build wealth by doing what everyone else does. Everyone else shops, spends, complains, and survives. If you want freedom, you must separate. But separation feels like betrayal to those still trapped, and that fear keeps many locked in the same cycle as their peers.

The Cost of Staying With the Crowd

When the crowd smokes, you smoke.

When the crowd overspends, you overspend.

When the crowd stays in the hood, you stay too.

When the crowd gives up, you give up.

The crowd is gravity. It pulls you down, even when you want to rise.

Corporate POV vs. Street POV

Corporate POV: Employees stay at dead-end jobs because “everyone else is staying.” They never challenge leadership, never start businesses, never invest differently. They fear being the one who takes a risk. The office crowd values safety over growth, and that safety keeps them all stuck.

Street POV: On the block, hustlers fear being called sellouts for leaving. They keep running the same corners, chasing the same fast money, even when prison or death is guaranteed. Those who break away are mocked until they succeed — then envied. But by then, the crowd is gone and the opportunity has passed.

Both sides reveal the same trap: loyalty to the crowd is loyalty to poverty.

The Psychology of Herd Fear

Psychologists call it “social conformity.” People adjust behavior to match the group, even when they know it’s wrong. Fear of rejection triggers the brain’s pain centers the same way physical pain does. That’s why leaving the crowd feels unbearable — but it’s the only path to change.

A Parable: The Sheep at the Cliff

A shepherd led sheep to a cliff. One by one, the sheep followed each other off the edge. Only one stopped, looked, and turned away. The flock mocked him, called him weak, called him different. But he lived. They died. Sometimes survival requires standing alone.

Case Study: The Entrepreneur vs. The Loyal Friend

Marcus and Jamal grew up in the same neighborhood. Both were smart, both had hustle. Marcus wanted to start a business, but Jamal mocked him: "That's corny, man. Just stick with us." Marcus left anyway, spent years grinding alone, and built a trucking company. Jamal stayed with the crew, loyal to the crowd. He's now serving twenty years. Marcus employs twenty drivers.

The difference wasn't talent. It was courage to leave.

Predictions if Unchecked

If fear of leaving the crowd continues, generations will keep recycling poverty. The ambitious will keep dimming their light to fit in. Communities will keep mocking their own leaders before outsiders even have to. And the few who dare to leave will carry the weight of envy and bitterness from those who stayed behind.

In twenty years, the wealth divide will look like this: a small group of individuals who dared to leave, and a massive crowd still stuck together, broke together.

Strategies to Break the Trap

Accept Isolation: Wealth requires seasons of loneliness. Prepare for it.

Find New Crowds: Don't just leave the old — join new circles of builders, thinkers, and doers.

Build Quietly: Don't argue with the crowd. Move in silence until results speak.

Redefine Loyalty: Be loyal to vision, not comfort.

Remember the Cliff: Following the crowd feels safe — until they all fall.

Closing Manifesto

You were not born to fit in. You were born to build. And building requires leaving. The crowd will call you selfish, arrogant, or disloyal. But their approval won't pay your bills, won't free your family, won't build your empire.

The crowd loves company, even in chains. Wealth requires separation. If you fear leaving, you fear living.

Walk away. Because the only thing waiting in the crowd is mediocrity.

Chapter 28 – Financial Illiteracy by Design

The Hidden Architecture of Ignorance

At the core of modern wealth inequality lies a simple truth: people are expected to navigate a complex financial landscape without ever being taught how

gflec.org

. Financial markets are packed with credit cards, mortgages, retirement accounts, payday loans, and investment vehicles. Yet schools rarely offer classes on compound interest, budgeting, taxes or credit management. This absence isn't accidental. As researchers Annamaria Lusardi and Olivia Mitchell point out, financial knowledge functions like human capital; differences in financial literacy lead directly to differences in wealth accumulation

gflec.org

. When people don't know how money works, they make choices that benefit lenders, retailers, and predators rather than themselves.

Financial illiteracy is often by design. Regulatory frameworks and industry lobbying keep personal finance off curricula, and communities with less political power—particularly low-income and marginalized groups—are left to learn about money through costly mistakes. Meanwhile, consumer finance grows increasingly sophisticated. Variable-rate loans, hidden fees, and complex insurance products require a level of understanding the average person doesn't have. Scholars show that inequality in wealth and financial knowledge arises endogenously; that is, wealth gaps expand without any differences in preferences, simply because some groups acquire financial skills while others don't

gflec.org

. This chapter exposes the systemic forces behind financial ignorance, illustrates its real-world consequences through corporate and street examples, and offers strategies to reclaim financial agency.

The Cost of Not Knowing

Ignorance is expensive. When you don't understand interest, you take loans with astronomical rates and pay the minimum for years, never touching the principal. When you don't grasp investment basics, you either avoid markets entirely or gamble on risky trends without diversification. Lack of financial literacy leads to poor budgeting, missing emergency funds, and vulnerability to scams. Scholars report that even small early investments in financial education generate enormous returns; providing pre-labor-market financial knowledge to less-educated workers can improve their wellbeing by the equivalent of 82 percent of their initial wealth

gflec.org

. That means money spent on financial education could yield more than almost any other investment—but most people never get the chance.

The cost isn't just individual. Entire communities lose millions because residents don't understand property taxes, insurance policies, or how to protect land titles.

Families who inherit homes without documentation lose them to foreclosure or predatory purchases because they don't know how to navigate the legal system. Unbanked households rely on payday lenders and check-cashing services that charge exorbitant fees. When citizens lack financial knowledge, economies suffer too—people spend more on debt service than on consumption or investment, limiting growth. Financial illiteracy acts as a tax on the poor and a subsidy for the wealthy.

Corporate POV vs. Street POV

Corporate Perspective

In the corporate world, financial literacy separates leaders from followers. Employees with high financial knowledge negotiate better compensation packages, leverage retirement plans, and understand the long-term benefits of stock options. They know the difference between a Roth and a traditional IRA, recognize how employer matches work, and avoid cashing out 401(k)s during job transitions. Conversely, workers without financial education often opt out of retirement plans, leave employer matches on the table, or withdraw savings with penalties to cover immediate needs. Companies benefit from employee ignorance; unclaimed benefits reduce costs, and high-interest company credit cards generate fees. On a larger scale, corporations design products that exploit consumer ignorance—teaser-rate mortgages, hidden surcharges, and loyalty programs that reward spending while masking the true cost.

Corporate boards and C-suite executives often come from backgrounds where financial literacy is taught at home or through elite education. They understand corporate finance, cost of capital, and investment strategy. This knowledge enables them to access cheap credit, structure businesses to minimize taxes, and grow wealth quickly. Employees further down the ladder rarely have access to such training, perpetuating a hierarchical knowledge gap.

Street Perspective

On the streets, financial illiteracy manifests differently but is just as deadly. A hustler with no understanding of pricing, overhead, or market dynamics underprices his product, mismanages cash flow, and ends up in debt or conflict. Communities that rely on informal economies often use money orders, prepaid cards, and cash transactions. Without bank accounts, they miss out on interest, credit-building, and transactional records that could be used to secure loans or prove income. The street entrepreneur might flip goods for quick cash but lacks a plan for scaling or transitioning to legitimate business because they don't know how to register an LLC, pay taxes, or apply for small business grants.

Predatory businesses thrive in these neighborhoods. Payday loan shops, rent-to-own furniture stores, and title loan outfits cluster where people lack financial knowledge. They advertise quick solutions and hidden fees, knowing most customers won't read the fine print. A man might pawn his car title for a few hundred dollars, then lose the car entirely when he can't keep up with triple-digit interest rates. A woman might finance a $500 sofa for $25 a week, paying double over time. On the block, ignorance can kill more effectively than bullets.

The Psychology of Financial Ignorance

Our brains aren't built for complex finance. Behavioral economists identify numerous cognitive biases that cause poor money decisions. Present bias makes immediate gratification more appealing than future benefits; that's why people spend tax refunds instead of saving them. Anchoring causes individuals to fixate on initial prices or rates, even when conditions change. Overconfidence leads to risky investments, while loss aversion prevents people from entering markets altogether. Without education to counteract these biases, individuals fall prey to marketing and psychological manipulation.

There's also cultural stigma. Talking about money is taboo in many households. Parents might shield children from financial stress to protect them, but in doing so, they never teach budgeting or planning. Schools avoid discussing money to prevent discomfort or because teachers themselves lack training. Communities sometimes reinforce the belief that wealth talk is "bourgeois," reinforcing skepticism about investing. These patterns create a self-perpetuating cycle where ignorance is inherited.

A Parable: The King and the Ledger

In a small kingdom, the king decreed that everyone must keep a ledger of their earnings and expenses. He provided instruction to the nobles, teaching them how to balance accounts and plan for the future. He did not teach the peasants, reasoning they did not handle enough money to need it. Years passed. The nobles grew wealthier; they invested surplus, lent money, and earned interest. The peasants lived hand to mouth, borrowing from the nobles and paying back more than they had borrowed. One day, a famine struck. The nobles had reserves and survived comfortably. The peasants starved, then revolted. The kingdom fell. The king realized too late that withholding knowledge had destroyed the realm he sought to control.

Case Studies: From Corporate Boardrooms to the Corner

The 401(k) Tragedy

Consider a corporate employee named Lisa. She earns $70,000 a year and works at a company that offers a 5 percent 401(k) match. Lisa never enrolls because she doesn't understand retirement plans. Over a decade, she misses out on $35,000 of employer contributions, plus investment growth. Her coworker, James, who took a finance class in college, contributes enough to maximize the match. When layoffs come, James has a sizable nest egg and options; Lisa has nothing. This scenario repeats across companies everywhere because financial literacy isn't universally taught.

Payday Prison

On the other side of town, Marcus lives paycheck to paycheck. When his car breaks down, he needs $500 immediately. Banks won't approve a loan because he has no credit history. A payday lender offers him $500 for a $75 fee, due in two weeks. Marcus thinks it's a good deal until he can't pay the full amount at once. He rolls the loan over, paying another $75. After six months, Marcus has paid $900 in fees—almost twice the original loan—without reducing the principal. If Marcus had known about credit unions or community loan funds, or had an emergency savings account, he could have avoided this trap. His ignorance feeds the payday lender's profit.

The Side Hustle Pivot

Jasmine, a street vendor selling homemade candles, initially prices them below cost because she doesn't calculate materials, time, or overhead. A local business mentor teaches her about cost analysis, pricing strategy, and bookkeeping. Jasmine raises prices, invests in branding, and opens an online store. She eventually transitions from a cash-based hustle to a registered business. Her income triples. The difference wasn't talent; it was knowledge.

Predictions if Unchecked

If financial illiteracy continues unchecked, wealth gaps will widen dramatically. Complex financial products will proliferate, and unscrupulous actors will exploit gaps in knowledge. People will accumulate debt they don't understand, sign away rights in contracts they can't read, and miss out on compound growth that could change their lives. Scholars predict that inequality in wealth and financial knowledge arises even without differences in preferences

gflec.org

. That means even if people want to save and invest, the lack of knowledge alone will keep them behind. Governments will shift more responsibility for retirement and healthcare costs onto individuals, further exposing those who lack financial literacy to risk

gflec.org

. Communities will remain dependent on low-wage jobs, and cycles of poverty will persist.

Moreover, the digitalization of finance means that those who can't navigate online banking, cryptocurrency platforms, and digital payments will be left out of mainstream commerce. Scams will become more sophisticated, targeting vulnerable populations with phishing, ransomware, and high-tech Ponzi schemes. Without intervention, the greatest wealth transfers in history—such as inheritances and stock market growth—will bypass those who don't know how to access them.

Strategies to Reclaim Financial Power

Financial literacy isn't a fixed trait; it's a skill set anyone can develop. Here are practical steps to break the trap:

Demand Education – Push schools, community centers, and workplaces to offer mandatory financial literacy courses. Research shows that early financial education delivers outsized benefits

gflec.org

.

Self-Study – Take ownership. There are countless free resources online: nonprofit websites, blogs, podcasts, and webinars. Start with budgeting, saving, and credit basics. Learn the differences between savings accounts, checking accounts, and investment vehicles. Understand compound interest, diversification, and inflation.

Join Financial Communities – Find or form investment clubs, credit unions, and community finance groups. Shared learning reduces intimidation. Local workshops often provide one-on-one counseling about debt management, mortgages, and small business financing.

Leverage Technology – Use budgeting apps, financial dashboards, and robo-advisors to gain insights into spending patterns and investment options. However, stay critical of fees and data privacy.

Protect Against Predators – Before signing any financial contract, read the fine print or consult someone who can. Avoid payday loans; look for community development financial institutions (CDFIs) or credit union small-dollar loans instead. Build an emergency fund to handle unexpected expenses without borrowing.

Teach the Next Generation – Break intergenerational cycles by openly discussing money at home. Involve children in budgeting and saving decisions. Show them how to compare prices, plan for future goals, and avoid impulse purchases.

Advocate for Policy Change – Support legislation that mandates financial education in schools, regulates predatory lending, and requires transparency in financial products. Vote for leaders who prioritize consumer protection.

Create and Save Documentation – Keep receipts, contracts, and statements organized. This builds a financial history that can help you qualify for loans and ensures you understand your obligations and rights.

Seek Professional Guidance – When possible, consult certified financial planners or credit counselors. Many offer sliding scales or pro bono services. A small investment in professional advice can save thousands later.

Practice Incremental Investing – Start small with index funds, mutual funds, or retirement accounts. Automate contributions. Compound interest grows significantly over time, and starting early matters more than the amount invested.

Closing Manifesto

Finance is not just for Wall Street. It is a language, a tool, a weapon. The system's greatest trick is convincing you it's too complicated for you to learn, that it's something only "experts" should handle. But scholars make clear that financial knowledge is simply human capital

gflec.org

. Like any skill, it can be acquired, and the benefits are immense. Early financial education can increase wellbeing by a magnitude equivalent to doubling wealth

gflec.org

. Left unchecked, financial illiteracy will continue to divide societies, locking millions into cycles of debt and poverty.

Reclaim your financial narrative. Read the books, take the courses, ask the questions. Demand transparency from those who design financial products. Teach your children what you were never taught. Build community networks that share information instead of gossip. Vote for policies that protect consumers and require schools to teach money management. Every person who learns how interest works, how to invest, how to budget, and how to read a contract becomes less exploitable and more powerful.

Ignorance is the enemy of freedom. Wealth does not come to those who wish for it; it comes to those who understand it. Break the silence. Break the cycle. Learn the rules, teach the rules, and bend them toward your liberation.

Chapter 29 – The Tax Trap

The Wealth Killer You Don't See Coming

Taxes are not neutral. They are the quietest, most consistent siphon of your life's energy. Every paycheck, every purchase, every property bill is touched by the hand of the state. You think you're keeping most of your money? You're not. Uncle Sam, the county, the state, the city, the hidden fees — they eat first. Always.

The rich call taxes a game. They hire lawyers, accountants, and lobbyists to twist laws in their favor. The poor call taxes a punishment, because for them it feels like there's no way out. But here's the bitter truth: if you don't learn the game of taxes, you will always be the ball getting kicked.

The tax trap isn't just income tax. It's sales tax, property tax, car tax, gas tax, capital gains tax, inflation tax, poverty fines, late fees, even the "black tax" of supporting family members who never escape their own traps. This isn't just numbers. This is how the system keeps wealth out of your hands.

The Layers of the Trap

Income Tax – You're taxed before you even see your money. The check that hits your account is already shaved.

Sales Tax – Every purchase, from sneakers to fast food, costs more than the sticker price.

Property Tax – You never truly own your home. Miss your property tax? Watch how fast the sheriff shows up.

Inflation Tax – The silent tax. Prices rise, your dollar buys less, and your savings rot while billionaires stash assets that grow faster than inflation.

Poverty Fines – Late fees, overdraft charges, traffic tickets. The poor get taxed more because they can't afford mistakes.

Generational Tax – Wealth passes down easily for the rich. For the poor, death taxes, probate costs, and lack of documentation eat whatever crumbs might've survived.

This trap is designed to feel "normal." That's why it works so well.

Corporate POV vs. Street POV
Corporate Perspective

Corporations don't fear taxes. They shape them.

Big companies hire lobbyists to write loopholes. That's why trillion-dollar corporations sometimes pay less tax than a janitor.

Billionaires don't "make money." They borrow against assets, avoid income, and play the tax code like a violin.

Every line of the tax code is a rulebook for how to avoid paying. And those who know the rules, win.

To corporations, taxes are just another business expense to negotiate down.

Street Perspective

On the block, taxes hit different.

The hustler pays “tax” to the system through constant fines, tickets, and fees.

A single mom’s paycheck gets chopped before it even lands, leaving her hustling side jobs just to cover groceries.

Neighborhoods with lower incomes pay higher percentages of their money in sales tax because they spend more on survival goods.

On the street, taxes feel like punishment for being broke.

The Psychology of the Tax Trap

Taxes don’t just take money — they shape how people think.

Learned Helplessness: People believe taxes are unavoidable, so they never try to learn the game.

Fear: People fear the IRS more than they fear poverty, so they never challenge unfairness.

Confusion: The system is designed to be complicated so regular people give up. Complexity is a weapon.

Normalization: Whole generations think "that's just how it is," never realizing others play by different rules.

The psychology of the tax trap keeps people compliant, obedient, and broke.

Parable: The Farmer's Harvest

A farmer worked hard all year, growing crops. At harvest, he filled 10 baskets. Just as he sat to enjoy the reward, a collector appeared. "Four baskets are mine." The farmer protested. The collector smiled, "That's the rule."

The next year, the farmer grew 12 baskets. The collector came again. "Six baskets are mine." The farmer's back broke under harder work, but no matter how much he grew, he never kept enough to get ahead. Eventually, the farmer realized: the harvest wasn't his. He was working someone else's land all along.

Case Studies

Wesley Snipes – Hollywood star, locked up not for violence or theft but for tax disputes. The IRS made an example of him to keep others compliant.

Amazon – Made billions, yet in multiple years paid close to zero federal income tax. They know the game.

Sharecropping 2.0 – After slavery, Black farmers were "taxed" through rigged rent, equipment fees, and crop liens. It looked legal, but it was theft in disguise.

Traffic Ticket Economy – In Ferguson, Missouri, city budgets depended heavily on fines and tickets — essentially taxing poverty to fund government.

Predictions if Unchecked

If the tax trap continues unchecked:

Widening Wealth Gaps: The rich will grow richer as they escape taxes, while the poor pay more of their shrinking income.

Digital Taxation: Cashless economies will allow governments to tax every micro-transaction in real time.

Climate of Fear: People will live in constant fear of audits and fees, never realizing that knowledge, not fear, is the true defense.

Modern Serfdom: People will never truly own property. Homes, cars, and businesses will all come with endless taxes attached — permanent rent to the system.

Strategies for Liberation

Study the Code: Tax codes aren't just rules for paying. They are instructions for avoiding. Learn them.

Get Documentation Right: Keep records, receipts, contracts. Paperwork is defense.

Shift from W-2 to 1099: Employees pay the most taxes. Entrepreneurs, contractors, and investors play by different rules.

Use LLCs and Trusts: Protect assets and create business expenses that reduce taxable income.

Invest, Don't Just Earn: Assets grow wealth without getting hit like wages do.

Community Education: Teach tax literacy in families and neighborhoods. Knowledge is leverage.

Challenge Poverty Fines: Fight back against predatory ticketing and fees through class actions, legal advocacy, and public exposure.

Closing Manifesto

The tax trap is not an accident. It is design. It is the hidden chain around every paycheck, every purchase, every dream. But chains can be broken.

The rich play the game, the poor pay the price. That's the truth. But if you learn the rules, you stop being a pawn. You stop feeding the beast. You stop working harder only to harvest less.

If you don't master taxes, taxes will master you.

Your enemy is not just poverty. It is the silent drain built into the system. And the only way to fight it is not with anger, but with knowledge, structure, and strategy. Because freedom is not just about having money — it's about keeping it.

Chapter 30 – Information Poverty

The Wealth Gap Nobody Talks About

Poverty isn't always about money. Sometimes it's about knowledge — or the lack of it. People don't just stay broke because they don't have cash. They stay broke because they don't know the rules, the resources, or the doors that already exist.

That's information poverty.

A millionaire might know about tax loopholes, offshore banking, grants, and investment strategies that never make it to the hood. A working-class family might qualify for government aid, business loans, or legal protections they never apply for — simply because nobody told them. The cruelest part? In the age of information, ignorance is no longer natural. It is engineered.

The Weaponization of Ignorance

The system doesn't just leave people uninformed. It profits off keeping people uninformed.

Legal Traps: Contracts are written in confusing language so the average person doesn't understand what they're signing.

Financial Traps: Banks bury fees and interest terms in fine print. People who don't read or can't interpret the details get drained.

Educational Gaps: Schools in poor neighborhoods rarely teach financial literacy, credit management, or business law.

Gatekeeping: Information is hidden behind paywalls, college degrees, or networks only the privileged can access.

The less you know, the more you pay. That's the design.

Corporate POV vs. Street POV
Corporate Perspective

Corporations see information as leverage.

Pharmaceuticals: Life-saving drug information is hidden in patents and legal jargon.

Tech Companies: They sell your data while keeping the mechanics secret.

Wall Street: They profit from complex systems the average person can't understand, from derivatives to hedge funds.

To corporations, confusion is a business model.

Street Perspective

On the street, information poverty shows up as mistakes that cost lives and legacies.

A man loses his house because he didn't know about property tax exemptions for veterans.

A single mom overpays utilities for years because she didn't know about assistance programs.

A young hustler signs away music rights for pennies because he doesn't understand publishing contracts.

On the street, ignorance is not bliss. It's bankruptcy.

The Psychology of Information Poverty

Information poverty isn't just about missing knowledge. It's about mindset.

Shame: People are embarrassed to admit what they don't know, so they never ask.

Mistrust: Years of exploitation make people suspicious of new information — even when it's real help.

Overwhelm: The flood of modern information makes people freeze. They can't filter truth from lies.

Resignation: Many believe "that's just not for us," internalizing exclusion as natural.

Psychological warfare keeps people from even reaching for the tools that exist.

Parable: The Locked Library

A village had a massive library filled with books on wealth, health, and freedom. But the door required a special key. The rich had the key and built dynasties. The poor walked past the library every day, believing it was empty. Generations later, the poor still struggled, never realizing the answers were there all along.

The library wasn't hidden. The key was.

Case Studies

The GI Bill Divide

After World War II, white veterans were given access to education and home loans. Black veterans were systematically excluded, not by lack of law but by lack of information and deliberate misdirection. Generations of wealth were lost.

Predatory Lending

Millions signed subprime mortgages before the 2008 crash. Why? Because they didn't understand adjustable rates or fine print. Banks knew they wouldn't.

Scholarships Unclaimed

Every year, billions in scholarship money goes unclaimed because students don't know it exists or how to apply. That's wealth left on the table.

Music Industry Exploitation

From Little Richard to TLC to modern rappers, countless artists signed contracts without legal knowledge. Hits made millions, but the creators stayed broke.

Predictions if Unchecked

If information poverty continues:

Wealth Gaps Grow: Knowledge-rich communities will accelerate, while others sink deeper.

Permanent Dependency: People will remain dependent on "experts" who charge for answers.

Digital Divide: As technology evolves, those without digital literacy will be locked out of entire economies.

Legacy Loss: Families will continue losing land, rights, and opportunities simply because they don't know the paperwork.

Ignorance isn't just costly. It's generational theft.

Strategies for Liberation

Normalize Asking Questions: Kill the shame. Teach that not knowing is temporary, but staying silent is permanent.

Build Community Libraries: Physical or digital hubs with resources on taxes, credit, health, and business.

Mentorship Chains: Those who know must teach those who don't. Knowledge only has power when it circulates.

Challenge Gatekeepers: Demand transparency in contracts, education, and government aid.

Use Free Resources: Public libraries, YouTube, online courses — knowledge exists, but discipline is needed to filter and apply it.

Teach Kids Early: Don't wait for schools. Families must pass down financial and legal literacy.

Paperwork Culture: Treat forms, receipts, and contracts like weapons. They are.

Closing Manifesto

Information poverty is the cruelest poverty of all, because the resources already exist. The doors are there. The keys are there. But if you don't know where to look, you will die outside the gate.

This system thrives on your ignorance. That's why schools don't teach wealth. That's why contracts are confusing. That's why help is hidden in fine print. But ignorance is not a curse. It's a condition. And conditions can change.

The day you decide to learn, ask, and document is the day you stop being prey.

Your freedom will not come from money first. It will come from knowledge. Because knowledge shapes money, multiplies money, and protects money.

In the age of information, ignorance is not just expensive — it is a choice.

Chapter 31 – The Social Media Mirage

The Digital Stage That Bankrupts the Soul

Social media was sold as a tool for connection. A way to share life, build networks, and create opportunity. But in practice, it's become the biggest illusion machine in history. It convinces broke people they're rich, lonely people they're popular, and distracted people that they're "in the know."

The problem isn't the tool. It's the addiction to the performance. Whole generations are trapped flexing for likes, chasing clout, and living in digital avatars while their real lives fall apart. This is the social media mirage: you look wealthy on the timeline, but your bank account says different. You look loved in the comments, but you're empty inside. You look productive online, but in the real world you're stuck.

The Trap of Digital Flex Culture

The mirage works because it feels real.

Clout Over Cash: People spend money they don't have to look rich on Instagram. Designer clothes, rented cars, fake vacations.

Validation Addiction: Every "like" is a dopamine hit. You start chasing approval like a drug.

Comparison Spiral: Seeing others' curated highlights makes you feel behind, even if it's all fake.

Time Drain: Hours lost posting, scrolling, editing, instead of building actual wealth.

Social media convinces you you're making moves while you're standing still.

Corporate POV vs. Street POV
Corporate Perspective

For corporations, social media is a goldmine.

Data Harvesting: Every like, comment, and share builds a profile they sell to advertisers.

Influencer Economy: They outsource advertising to regular people hungry for clout. The influencers flex, the corporations profit.

Consumer Traps: Ads target your insecurities, pushing products the second you feel envy.

Social media is not free. You pay with your time, your data, and your mind.

Street Perspective

On the street, the mirage is devastating.

Young hustlers waste money flexing with props instead of investing in tools.

Women chase influencer lifestyles, spending on hair, clothes, and trips for digital approval.

Men throw rent money at bottle service just to look like "ballers" for one night on Snapchat.

The block becomes a stage. Real life becomes a shadow.

The Psychology of the Mirage

Social media is engineered to manipulate psychology.

Fear of Missing Out (FOMO): Platforms show what "everyone" is doing so you feel left out.

Dopamine Dependency: Likes and shares trigger the same brain chemicals as drugs.

Ego Inflation: You build an online persona that feels bigger than your real self.

Identity Confusion: You start living for the avatar instead of the actual you.

This psychology keeps people locked in cycles of distraction and spending.

Parable: The Digital Oasis

A traveler dying of thirst walked the desert. In the distance, he saw water shimmering. He ran toward it, desperate for life. But when he arrived, the water vanished. It was a mirage — beautiful from afar, empty up close.

He collapsed in the sand, chasing illusions while the real well was behind him all along.

Case Studies

Fyre Festival

An entire luxury event was sold on Instagram by influencers. Thousands bought tickets to a paradise that never existed. Social media sold the dream; reality was disaster.

Rapper Contracts

Countless rappers flex millions in music videos while still locked in deals that leave them broke. The label funds the image, but owns the profit.

Influencer Burnout

Many influencers admit to depression, debt, and exhaustion behind the scenes. The curated lifestyle hides the real pain.

Everyday Flexers

People max out credit cards for vacations, jewelry, or cars just to post pictures. The likes vanish in days. The debt remains for years.

Predictions if Unchecked

If the social media mirage continues:

Debt Epidemics: More young people will go broke chasing digital status.

Mental Health Collapse: Depression, anxiety, and envy will skyrocket.

Shallow Culture: Real skills, work, and growth will lose value against clout.

Control by Algorithms: The more you feed the avatar, the less you own your real self.

Whole generations risk living and dying for an audience instead of a legacy.

Strategies for Liberation

Separate Avatar From Reality: Social media is a tool, not an identity.

Audit Your Timeline: Unfollow content that feeds envy, flexing, or distraction.

Build Offline Wealth: Spend more hours building assets than building posts.

Monetize, Don't Just Scroll: If you're online, turn content into income, not just attention.

Digital Detox: Step away to reset your brain's reward system.

Teach Youth Early: Show kids the difference between image and reality before the trap grabs them.

Reclaim Community: Build reputation in real life, where it actually pays dividends.

Closing Manifesto

The social media mirage is the new plantation. The whip isn't physical — it's digital envy, likes, and comparison. Millions are enslaved by the need to look wealthy instead of becoming wealthy.

But mirages don't have to control you. You can stop chasing illusions and start digging real wells. You can build assets, skills, and communities that don't disappear when the Wi-Fi cuts off.

Stop living for the feed. Start living for the legacy.

Because the truth is simple: clout won't pay your bills. Likes won't leave your kids an inheritance. And an online persona won't protect you from poverty.

Only real wealth, built in the real world, will.

Chapter 32 – Health Hustlers

The Price of Sickness in a System That Profits From Pain

Wealth isn't just about money. It's about health. Without energy, without stamina, without a functioning body, you can't build or sustain wealth. And the darker truth? The health industry doesn't exist to heal you. It exists to keep you sick enough to spend.

The hustlers of health wear white coats, run billion-dollar corporations, and smile on commercials. They don't stand on street corners, but they're still pushing product — prescriptions, surgeries, "miracle" diets, supplements, and procedures. They don't just sell pills. They sell dependency.

This is the health hustle: when your body becomes a profit center and your sickness is someone else's income stream.

The Design of the Health Trap

The health system doesn't just fail the poor. It preys on them.

Prescription Addiction – Doctors over-prescribe opioids, antidepressants, and pills that treat symptoms but never cure the root.

Food Industry Collusion – Junk food is marketed heavy in poor neighborhoods, fueling diabetes, heart disease, and obesity.

Insurance Hustle – Premiums rise, coverage shrinks. You pay for "protection" you can't afford to use.

Preventive Neglect – Systems focus on treating sickness, not preventing it. Why? Prevention kills profit.

Generational Drain – Families lose savings caring for elders in broken systems while billion-dollar corporations grow fat off suffering.

The health hustle is one of the most expensive wealth killers in existence.

Corporate POV vs. Street POV
Corporate Perspective

Pharmaceuticals: Drugs are priced at 100x production costs. Why cure diseases when lifelong treatment is more profitable?

Food Giants: Addictive sugar, salt, and fat are pumped into products, then marketed as "convenience."

Insurance Companies: Billions in revenue come not from saving lives but from denying coverage.

Hospitals: Charge $50 for aspirin, $10,000 for ambulance rides. Profit first, healing second.

Corporations see human bodies as cash cows. Sickness is a subscription model.

Street Perspective

On the block, the health hustle is brutal.

Fast food chains saturate poor neighborhoods, while organic groceries are miles away.

People delay checkups because they can’t afford the co-pay. By the time they go, it’s too late.

Hustlers push street remedies — cheap liquor, weed, pills — as escape from untreated stress and trauma.

Families bury loved ones early because healthcare came too late, too expensive, or too biased.

The poor die younger not because of genes, but because of systems designed to hustle their health.

The Psychology of the Hustle

Health hustlers play the long game by manipulating psychology.

Fear: Scare tactics push people into unnecessary procedures.

Addiction: Processed foods and pills are engineered to create dependency.

Convenience Culture: Busy, broke people choose fast fixes over long-term health.

Denial: People avoid facing health issues because the system feels overwhelming and hostile.

This cycle keeps people docile, tired, and broke.

Parable: The Healer and the Merchant

In an old village, two men offered cures. The healer sold herbs that required patience and discipline but cured sickness at the root. The merchant sold bright-colored potions that made people feel better instantly but created new problems later. The villagers chose the merchant because his solution was fast. Soon the whole village depended on him — sick, weak, and broke.

The healer starved. The merchant thrived.

Case Studies

Opioid Epidemic

Pharmaceutical giants knowingly fueled an addiction crisis, marketing opioids as “safe” while raking in billions. Communities were destroyed. Executives walked away rich.

Tuskegee Experiment

Black men were denied treatment for syphilis so doctors could “study the disease.” Health was sacrificed for exploitation.

Food Deserts

Millions live in areas with no access to fresh groceries, forced into fast food diets that guarantee long-term disease.

Insulin Pricing

In the U.S., insulin costs up to 10x more than in other countries. People literally die rationing medicine that costs pennies to produce.

Predictions if Unchecked

If the health hustle continues:

Shorter Lifespans: Poor communities will keep dying younger while the rich live decades longer.

Debt Through Illness: Families will sink into medical debt that outlives the patient.

Bio-Slavery: Genetic data and personalized medicine will be monetized, creating a new class system based on health access.

Permanent Fatigue: Entire populations will stay too tired and sick to resist or build.

The hustlers will grow richer. The people will grow weaker.

Strategies for Liberation

Preventive Lifestyle: Treat exercise, sleep, and diet like wealth investments.

Food Awareness: Cook at home. Read labels. Understand how food is engineered.

Alternative Medicine: Explore safe natural remedies and practices outside the pharmaceutical monopoly.

Community Clinics: Build grassroots health resources where systems fail.

Demand Accountability: Expose and resist predatory practices in pharmaceuticals and insurance.

Health as Discipline: Treat your body like an asset. Maintenance is wealth protection.

Generational Teaching: Pass health wisdom to children so cycles break early.

Closing Manifesto

Health hustlers are the most dangerous wealth killers because they rob you of the one thing you can't replace: time in your body. They turn your flesh into finance, your pain into profit, your sickness into someone else's inheritance.

But you don't have to play their game. You can resist the hustle by building strength, discipline, and awareness. You can refuse to be a permanent patient. You can reclaim the power of prevention, the wisdom of self-care, and the community of collective health.

Because wealth without health is nothing. And health without independence is slavery.

Stop feeding the health hustlers. Start feeding yourself.

Chapter 33 – The Silence of Networking

Closed Mouths Don't Build Kingdoms

You've heard the saying: closed mouths don't get fed. That's not just about hunger — it's about wealth. Opportunities move through people. Doors open because of connections. Networks are ladders. And yet, too many people stay silent. They avoid networking, refuse to ask for help, or only speak to the wrong people. That silence doesn't just cost conversations. It costs futures.

Networking is not begging. Networking is currency. Your reputation, your introductions, your relationships are as powerful as money in the bank. But when you avoid the room, skip the call, burn the bridge, or stay invisible, you guarantee your ceiling.

The silence of networking is a wealth killer because no one builds empires alone.

The Trap of Isolation

Here's how silence sabotages wealth:

Fear of Rejection – People would rather stay quiet than risk hearing "no."

Pride – Some think asking for help looks weak.

Comfort Zones – Talking only to family or friends who can't elevate you.

Burnt Bridges – Gossip, envy, or immaturity destroy potential connections.

One-Sidedness – Only reaching out when you need something, instead of building consistent value.

Isolation feels safe, but it's actually suffocation.

Corporate POV vs. Street POV

Corporate Perspective

In corporate America, networking isn't optional. It's strategy.

Executives golf with partners, trade favors, and secure billion-dollar deals off the clock.

Hiring Managers often fill roles through referrals before jobs even post.

Investors back people they know, not strangers with great ideas.

Corporations thrive on networks. It's not what you know — it's who you know and who knows you.

Street Perspective

On the street, silence hurts too.

A hustler doesn't move product without connections.

Local artists die broke because they never build ties with promoters, investors, or producers.

Communities miss grants and resources because nobody knew who to call or how to ask.

Networking on the street can mean survival, but silence means stagnation.

The Psychology of Silence

Networking isn't just about skill — it's about mindset.

Low Self-Worth: People who don't believe they're valuable won't step into the room.

Trauma of Rejection: Past failures haunt new opportunities.

Imposter Syndrome: Feeling unworthy of powerful connections.

Survival Thinking: Focus on today's problems leaves no bandwidth for building relationships that pay off tomorrow.

Psychology keeps people muted, even when their future depends on speaking up.

Parable: The Quiet Merchant

Two merchants sold goods in the same market. One shouted loudly, telling everyone about his wares. The other stayed quiet, believing “the right people will find me.” Years passed. The loud merchant built wealth and expanded. The quiet one starved, his stall invisible in the crowd.

The difference wasn’t quality. It was silence.

Case Studies

Silicon Valley Founders

Many billion-dollar startups weren’t built by the smartest engineers, but by those who networked into funding circles. Talent without networking stalls.

Black Wall Street Survivors

Even after Tulsa’s massacre, survivors rebuilt through tight community networks. Wealth flowed because connections stayed strong.

Corporate Promotions

Studies show 85% of jobs are filled through networking. That means silence costs careers.

Music Industry

Unsigned artists with raw talent remain unknown, while mediocre artists with strong networks thrive.

Predictions if Unchecked

If silence continues to dominate:

Generational Stagnation: Families will stay stuck because they don't know how to tap networks for opportunity.

Community Decay: Neighborhoods will lose resources to outsiders who simply knew who to ask.

Talent Waste: Brilliant ideas will die in notebooks while average ideas win, just because someone spoke up.

Permanent Outsider Status: Those without networks will always be workers, never owners.

Silence doesn't just cost moments. It costs dynasties.

Strategies for Liberation

Shift the Mindset: Networking isn't begging. It's trading value.

Be Present in Rooms: Show up where decisions happen, not just where you're comfortable.

Follow Up: Don't just meet people — maintain the connection.

Give First: Offer value before asking for it. Relationships must be mutual.

Bridge Building: Heal old conflicts and stop burning potential allies.

Digital Networking: Use platforms like LinkedIn, but push conversations into real calls and meetings.

Teach Kids Early: Train children that confidence and connection are tools as important as education.

Closing Manifesto

Closed mouths don't build wealth. Silence doesn't protect you — it erases you. In a world where opportunities move through people, refusing to speak is refusing to succeed.

The silence of networking is a silent coffin. You bury your potential while watching louder, less talented people win. But the solution is simple: open your mouth, step into the room, ask the question, make the call, follow up.

Because in this world, your network is your net worth. And if you don't build one, you'll always work for someone who did.

Chapter 34 – Overeducation Without Application

Degrees Without Direction

Education is supposed to be the great equalizer. That's the dream we were sold: get the degree, and the world will open its doors. But in reality, education without application is one of the biggest wealth killers of modern times. People stack degrees, certifications, and credentials — and yet they're broke, jobless, or trapped under crushing debt.

The problem isn't learning. Learning is power. The problem is mistaking paper for practice, status for strategy. The system told you more school equals more success, while quietly rigging the game so your degree doesn't guarantee opportunity. Overeducation without application is chasing knowledge without building value. It's climbing a ladder that leans against the wrong wall.

The Trap of Endless Schooling

Here's how it plays out:

Debt Overload – Students borrow tens of thousands — sometimes hundreds of thousands — for degrees that don't pay back.

Misdirected Learning – People study theory but never gain practical skills.

Overqualification – Some get degrees that make them "too educated" for entry-level jobs but not specialized enough for advanced ones.

Credential Chasing – Certificates stacked like trophies, but none connected to a business, hustle, or applied project.

Deferred Living – People spend their 20s and 30s in classrooms while peers build wealth and experience.

The trap isn't education itself. It's worshiping credentials while starving application.

Corporate POV vs. Street POV

Corporate Perspective

Colleges: Sell degrees like products. The more students enroll, the more they profit, regardless of job placement.

Employers: Use degrees as filters, not guarantees. A piece of paper doesn't mean you can execute.

Banks: Profit from student loans, locking people into decades of repayment.

Corporations see education as an industry, not empowerment.

Street Perspective

On the street, the hustle looks different.

Kids are told "college is the only way out," while trades, entrepreneurship, and skills are ignored.

Families push degrees as proof of success, even if the graduate ends up broke and stressed.

Whole communities worship letters after names while overlooking those who applied fewer skills but built more wealth.

On the block, overeducation without application feels like betrayal. You did everything "right," and still ended up stuck.

The Psychology of the Trap

Fear of Falling Behind: People keep going back to school because they're scared of being outdated.

Status Addiction: Families and communities praise degrees, so people chase validation instead of outcomes.

Avoidance: School becomes a way to delay real-world responsibility.

Illusion of Security: Degrees feel safe in a world of uncertainty, but safety is often a lie.

Psychology fuels the cycle of learning without earning.

Parable: The Collector of Keys

A man wanted to open the door to wealth. He collected keys from every market, teacher, and village. His house filled with keys of all shapes and colors. But when he reached the door, he realized none of them fit — because he never studied the lock.

He had keys without purpose. Knowledge without application.

Case Studies

Student Debt Crisis

In the U.S., student debt exceeds $1.7 trillion. Millions owe more than they can ever repay, degrees or not.

MBA Graduates

Some MBA grads earn six figures, but many others end up unemployed or underpaid because the market is saturated.

Trades vs. Degrees

Plumbers, electricians, and mechanics often out-earn degree holders, with far less debt.

PhD Poverty

Many PhDs work as adjunct professors, paid less than fast-food managers, while buried in debt from a decade of schooling.

Predictions if Unchecked

If overeducation without application continues:

Debt Slavery: Generations will be financially paralyzed by loans.

Devaluation of Degrees: More degrees will mean less value, as employers look for proof of skill instead of paper.

Skill Gaps: People will leave school unprepared for real-world innovation.

Generational Misdirection: Families will keep pressuring youth into debt traps that don't lead to wealth.

Strategies for Liberation

Shift the Focus: Education must be about skills and application, not status.

Learn Trades and Tech: High-demand skills often pay more than degrees.

Pair Knowledge with Hustle: Apply lessons through businesses, side hustles, and projects.

Question the Path: Don't go to school just because it's expected. Calculate ROI like an investment.

Use Free Learning: Online resources, mentorships, and apprenticeships can outdo overpriced degrees.

Community Awareness: Stop worshiping degrees as proof of success. Measure by impact, not credentials.

Teach ROI Early: Show kids the financial consequences of student debt before they sign.

Closing Manifesto

Education is power — but only if applied. Degrees without direction are just expensive trophies. The system profits when you worship paper, not practice. And the streets suffer when potential is buried under debt and delay.

Knowledge is not the goal. Application is. Action is. Wealth doesn't come from what you know. It comes from what you do with what you know.

Stop collecting keys that don't open doors. Learn the lock. Build the door if you have to. Apply the knowledge until it pays dividends.

Because the truth is simple: overeducation without application is not empowerment. It's enslavement with a cap and gown.

Chapter 35 – Survival Mode Thinking

Living to Get By, Not to Get Ahead

Survival is natural. It's instinct. Every living thing fights to eat, breathe, and protect itself. But when survival becomes a permanent mindset, it kills wealth before it can even be born. Survival mode keeps people trapped in cycles where the only focus is "right now." Tomorrow doesn't exist. Next year doesn't matter. Generational wealth? That's a fantasy when you're just trying to keep the lights on.

Survival mode thinking is dangerous because it feels justified. Bills are due. Kids need food. Rent is late. But living in constant survival rewires the brain. It makes you reactive instead of strategic. And wealth only grows through strategy, patience, and long-term vision.

The Trap of Survival Mode

Survival thinking has predictable patterns:

Short-Term Hustles – Taking quick cash jobs or side hustles that never scale.

Consumption Over Investment – Spending on instant relief instead of long-term growth.

Risk Aversion – Too scared to invest or try new ventures because failure feels fatal.

Panic Decisions – Making financial choices out of fear instead of analysis.

Generational Stagnation – Teaching children survival habits instead of wealth-building habits.

Survival mode makes poverty feel permanent.

Corporate POV vs. Street POV
Corporate Perspective

Corporations know survival mode is profitable.

Payday Loans: Exploit desperation with sky-high interest rates.

Fast Food Chains: Offer cheap relief that destroys long-term health.

Gig Economy: Companies profit when workers accept scraps just to make it through the week.

Retail Stores: Push buy-now-pay-later schemes that keep people in cycles of debt.

Corporate America thrives on people who can't think past Friday.

Street Perspective

On the street, survival mode is visible every day.

Hustlers flip quick money but never build real assets.

People rent forever, too focused on bills to save for property.

Neighborhoods normalize check-to-check living, making wealth seem unreachable.

Violence spikes when people fight for scraps because no one's thinking long-term.

Survival is respected, but it rarely builds escape.

The Psychology of Survival

Survival thinking is hardwired into the brain by stress and scarcity.

Cortisol Flood: Constant stress hormones reduce focus, memory, and decision-making.

Tunnel Vision: The brain narrows in on immediate threats, ignoring long-term solutions.

Scarcity Loop: People overvalue small gains now while undervaluing larger gains later.

Trauma: Generational poverty creates mindsets where abundance feels impossible.

It's not just mindset. It's biology turned against you.

Parable: The Two Hunters

Two hunters were given bows. One hunted rabbits every day, bringing home scraps. The other built traps, studied the land, and waited weeks to catch a deer. The rabbit hunter always ate but never more than enough. The deer hunter starved at first but later fed his whole tribe.

Both men had the same tools. Their thinking made the difference.

Case Studies

Lottery Winners

Many broke people who suddenly hit jackpots lose everything within years. Why? Survival habits, not wealth habits. They think short-term, so the money vanishes.

2008 Financial Crisis

Millions took bad mortgages because the short-term "low payments" seemed manageable. Survival thinking blinded them to long-term traps.

Hustle Culture

Artists, workers, and hustlers burn out chasing daily bread without ever building systems that create passive wealth.

Great Depression Families

Some families never recovered because their survival habits became generational. Even decades later, descendants lived as if collapse was still right around the corner.

Predictions if Unchecked

If survival mode thinking dominates:

Permanent Underclass: Whole communities will stay stuck, unable to break cycles of poverty.

Burnout Epidemics: People will collapse from exhaustion, never reaching stability.

Wealth Concentration: Strategic thinkers will keep consolidating resources while survival thinkers stay on the treadmill.

Generational Hopelessness: Children raised in survival mode will repeat the same patterns, believing wealth is "for other people."

Survival without escape becomes slavery.

Strategies for Liberation

Shift Mindset: Treat survival as a phase, not a lifestyle.

Build Buffers: Emergency savings break the panic cycle.

Plan Small, Think Big: Even small investments compound when directed strategically.

Learn Delayed Gratification: Value tomorrow's wealth more than today's relief.

Skill Building: Trade some hustle time for learning skills that elevate earning power.

Community Wealth: Pool resources with trusted networks to break isolation.

Therapy and Healing: Address trauma so survival doesn't become identity.

Closing Manifesto

Survival mode is necessary in crisis, but deadly as a lifestyle. It keeps you chasing rabbits when deer are possible. It keeps you reactive, tired, and trapped in cycles that feel permanent.

The truth is simple: you can't build wealth while stuck in survival. You must break the cycle by thinking past today, past this week, past this year. You must plan for a future that feels impossible while surviving a present that feels unbearable.

Because survival alone doesn't equal freedom. It equals captivity with food on the table.

Choose strategy over panic. Choose investment over relief. Choose the long game over the short hustle. Because survival may keep you alive, but vision is what makes you free.

Chapter 36 – The Scarcity Identity

When Poverty Becomes a Personality

Scarcity isn't just about what you don't have. It's about what you believe you'll never have. Scarcity identity is when lack becomes your lifestyle, when "not enough" becomes who you are. People stuck in scarcity don't just live in poverty — they internalize it, wear it, and pass it down like inheritance.

The most dangerous part? Scarcity identity is invisible to the person carrying it. They think they're being "realistic." They think they're "humble." But in truth, they're rehearsing poverty every day with their words, their habits, their decisions, and their mindset. And wealth can never exist where lack is worshiped as truth.

The Anatomy of Scarcity Identity

Scarcity identity shows up in predictable ways:

Language of Lack – Always saying "I can't afford that," "That's for them, not us," or "Money doesn't grow on trees."

Fear of Abundance – Rejecting opportunities because they "sound too good to be true."

Penny Pinching, Dollar Losing – Saving small but ignoring big investments that build wealth.

Crab-in-a-Barrel Syndrome – Competing with each other for scraps instead of collaborating for abundance.

Generational Programming – Kids inherit the same scarcity mindsets, even if circumstances change.

Scarcity identity doesn't just live in wallets. It lives in words, beliefs, and habits.

Corporate POV vs. Street POV
Corporate Perspective

Corporations exploit scarcity psychology daily.

Advertising: "Limited time only." "While supplies last." They manufacture scarcity to make you spend faster.

Pay Structures: Employers keep wages low so workers stay dependent.

Consumer Loans: Scarcity makes people desperate for payday loans, credit cards, and buy-now-pay-later traps.

Corporations know people who believe in scarcity are easy to control.

Street Perspective

On the block, scarcity identity is a badge.

People flex to hide lack, spending their last on shoes while rent's unpaid.

Neighborhoods fight each other over small opportunities while outsiders buy up the land.

Families discourage ambition: "Don't get your hopes up." "That ain't for us."

Community gossip shames those who dare to dream bigger.

Scarcity identity feels like culture, but it's actually chains.

The Psychology of Scarcity

Scarcity doesn't just limit finances. It rewires the brain.

Tunnel Vision: Focus narrows to immediate problems, blocking long-term strategy.

Risk Aversion: People avoid opportunities because failure feels fatal.

Comparison Addiction: People obsess over what others have, deepening envy and hopelessness.

Low Self-Worth: Scarcity convinces people they don't deserve more, so they never try.

It's not just poverty. It's poverty turned into personality.

Parable: The Beggar's Bowl

A beggar sat with a small bowl, collecting coins. A stranger offered him a pot big enough to feed his whole family. The beggar refused. "This bowl is all I know. If I take more, I'll lose what I have." He died with a half-full bowl, never realizing the pot was his way out.

Scarcity didn't just kill his wealth. It killed his vision.

Case Studies

Sharecropping Mindset

Even after slavery, Black farmers accepted unfair deals because they couldn't imagine land ownership. Scarcity was normalized.

Immigrant Hustles

Some immigrant groups pooled resources, while others stayed locked in survival competition. Collaboration vs. scarcity shaped their generational outcomes.

Lottery Winners Again

Winners who grew up in scarcity often lose it all. Why? Because their mindset couldn't stretch to abundance. They went broke trying to fill an identity rooted in lack.

Corporate Employees

Workers who never ask for raises or promotions because they fear rejection — scarcity identity disguised as humility.

Predictions if Unchecked

If scarcity identity dominates:

Generational Poverty: Families will pass down poverty not just in dollars, but in beliefs.

Wealth Transfer Failure: Even when money arrives, it will be mismanaged and lost.

Exploitation Intensifies: Corporations will keep milking scarcity-driven consumers.

Cultural Stagnation: Communities will celebrate survival instead of success.

Scarcity identity makes freedom impossible because the prison lives inside the mind.

Strategies for Liberation

Change Language: Replace "I can't afford it" with "How can I afford it?"

Practice Abundance: Surround yourself with people, books, and experiences that expand vision.

Collaborate, Don't Compete: Pool resources, share knowledge, build together.

Take Calculated Risks: Learn that failure is part of growth, not proof of lack.

Teach Kids Differently: Stop programming scarcity phrases into their vocabulary.

Expose Yourself: Travel, network, and study outside your bubble to expand possibility.

Shift Identity: Don't call yourself broke. Call yourself building.

Closing Manifesto

Scarcity identity is the most dangerous wealth killer because it convinces you to guard your chains. It makes you comfortable in lack. It teaches you to protect the very mindset that keeps you enslaved.

But poverty is not a personality. It's a condition — and conditions can change.

You are not scarcity. You are potential.

The moment you shift from lack to abundance, everything changes. Because wealth isn't just about money.

It's about identity. And if you never see yourself as worthy of abundance, you will never touch it.

Scarcity says, "This is all there is." Abundance says, "This is just the beginning." The choice is yours.

Closing Manifesto – No More Silent Deaths of Wealth

You've walked through the shadows. You've seen the killers. And the hardest truth of all is this: they were never hiding. They lived in your daily choices. They lived in your body, your habits, your conversations, your silence. They sat at your dinner table, slept in your bed, stared back at you from the mirror.

The system didn't need to chain you with whips — it chained you with distractions, insecurities, blind obedience, emotional spending, gossip, comfort, and fear. It taught you to survive while never teaching you to build. It fed you debt instead of discipline, loyalty to crowds instead of loyalty to purpose, entertainment instead of education.

Wealth was never just about money. It was about vision. It was about health. It was about discipline. It was about the courage to leave the crowd, the hunger to keep learning, the boldness to ask the right people for help, and the wisdom to document your path. Every silent killer we exposed in these chapters is a parasite — feeding on your potential, bleeding your future, and leaving you wondering why nothing ever changes.

But now you know. And once you know, you can't unknow.

The closing line of defense is you. Not your boss. Not your parents. Not politicians. Not even your pastor. You. Every wealth killer in this book can be starved the moment you decide to stop feeding it. Your habits, your time, your relationships, your health, your imagination — these are the engines of your future net worth. Guard them like treasure.

Understand this: nobody is coming to save you. The cavalry isn't on the way. But you have something stronger — the ability to rebuild yourself into the type of person who cannot be trapped. If you heal your inner child, discipline your body, protect your time, feed your curiosity, and master financial literacy, you become untouchable.

And once you become untouchable, you become unstoppable.

This is more than a book. It's a call to arms. Every chapter ends with a manifesto because every day you live with these killers unchallenged is another day of slavery in disguise. You are not here to simply exist. You are here to build, to rise, to leave behind a blueprint so solid that your children and their children never again have to fight these same invisible enemies.

Wealth is not just dollars stacked in banks. Wealth is freedom. Wealth is choice. Wealth is health. Wealth is reputation. Wealth is time. Wealth is documented legacy that nobody can erase.

Kill the killers before they kill your future.

From this day forward, let every dollar, every hour, every relationship, and every decision be a soldier fighting for your liberation. Let your imagination outrun your fear. Let your curiosity outlive your comfort. Let your strategy outlast their traps.

Because the truth is brutal, but it is also beautiful:

You were never broke because you lacked money. You were broke because you let silent killers steal your potential. Starve them, and you starve poverty itself.

The time for survival is over. The era of building begins now.

About the Author

Patrice Shabazz is a son of North Carolina — raised by hardship, hardened by experience, and healed through truth. A sharp voice forged in poverty, he writes to expose the systems that keep everyday people buried under debt, silence, and struggle. His words don't just teach — they testify.

Patrice's mission reaches beyond the page. He is actively working to build a self-sustainable community rooted in group economics, accountability, and liberation. Through books, outreach, and strategic action, he's not just telling stories — he's blueprinting solutions.

If you are a like-minded individual, a builder, a visionary, or simply someone curious about how we rise together, reach out: patriceshabazz39@gmail.com

---

"A lone runner may reach the hill first — but a village crosses mountains."

— Patrice Shabazz

Led by Patrice Shabazz | Founder, Exclusive Heights

We're building more than a neighborhood — we're building a future.

The Vision

Imagine 300–500 acres of land, powered by solar, growing our own food, raising livestock, creating jobs, and raising children in a safe, educated, self-governed environment.

This isn't a dream. This is a blueprint.

We're forming a 1,000-person self-sustainable Black-led community rooted in:

- Group economics
- Cooperative living
- Clean food, clean water, clean energy
- Vocational training & land-based education
- Mental, physical, and financial healing

———

The Math & Mission

- Goal: $12,000 per person x 1,000 = $12 million
- Covers: Land (300–500 acres), infrastructure, housing, farming, solar, schools, tradespaces, and startup capital for community-owned businesses.

Every dollar goes into ownership, food security, and generational wealth — not rent.

———

Who We're Looking For

We're recruiting:

- Skilled tradespeople: Electricians, Plumbers, Builders, Farmers, HVAC, Welders
- Educators & Mentors: Teachers, Counselors, Homeschoolers, Youth Leaders
- Medical & Holistic Health: Nurses, CNAs, Herbalists, Wellness Coaches
- Tech & Media: Web Designers, Editors, Content Creators
- General Builders: Visionaries willing to work, grow, and invest in change

———

Why Join?

- Be part of a legacy project
- Live and work with purpose
- Help build Black independence
- Escape survival mode and enter sustainability
- Your name will be on the foundation of a new nation within a nation

———

Support & Donate

Help fund the first phase:

- [GoFundMe gofund.me/637427e2]
- Cash App: $ExclusiveHeights

Every donation brings us one step closer to land, infrastructure, and freedom.

———

Get Involved

Contact: patriceshabazz39@gmail.com
Based in North Carolina — open to national collaboration

———

"A system built to bury us… won't survive the ones who plant back."
— Patrice Shabazz

Made in the USA
Monee, IL
05 November 2026

68020972R00146